BRITISH FOREIGN SECRETARIES SINCE 1945
Peter Jones, Keith Sainsbury & Avi Shlaim

'. . . should interest the general reader . . . because it deals with politicians of the comparatively recent past or the present — Ernest Bevin to Alec Home.' —*Daily Telegraph*

'This collection of essays, the product of the department of politics in the University of Reading, is impressive . . . they are very ready to make overall and controversial judgements about the men whose work they are examining.' — *New Society*
216 x 138mm

KINGS AND QUEENS OF ENGLAND AND GREAT BRITAIN
Devised and edited by Eric R. Delderfield

A popular summary of the principal dates, happenings and accomplishments of the monarchs of England and Great Britain.
227 x 131mm   Illustrated

PRESIDENTS OF THE USA
Denys Cook

A study especially prepared for the non-American reader, amounting to an indispensable source of interest and information on the men, the office and the nation.
216 x 138mm

PRIME MINISTERS OF BRITAIN
Eileen Hellicar

From Sir Robert Walpole to James Callaghan, forty-eight men have held the office of Prime Minister. In this book, Eileen Hellicar lifts the mask to show the men behind the title, relates the events of their careers, the deeds that made them famous or the blunders that brought them down, and shows how the original opinions of them have been re-assessed over the years.
216 x 138mm   Illustrated

BUT WHO ON EARTH WAS...?

Eileen Hellicar

BUT WHO ON EARTH WAS...?

DAVID & CHARLES

Newton Abbot   London   North Pomfret (Vt)

FOR MY PARENTS

I should like to thank Shirley Curzon for drawing the portraits, Daisy Hellicar for compiling the index, Sue Roberts for her professional help in the research and Audrey Tapley for typing the manuscript.

British Library Cataloguing in Publication Data

Hellicar, Eileen
  But who on earth was ...?
  1. Biography—Juvenile literature
  I. Title
  920'.02   CT107
  ISBN 0-7153-7962-3
  Library of Congress Catalog Card
  Number 80-85492

Typeset and printed in Great Britain
by Butler & Tanner Ltd, Frome and London
for David & Charles (Publishers) Limited
Brunel House Newton Abbot Devon

Published in the United States of America
by David & Charles Inc
North Pomfret   Vermont 05053   USA

Contents

Introduction

*There be of them, that have left a
name behind*
(Ecclesiasticus)

WHO IS SO NONCHALANT that he is not inquisitive about a name, strange or otherwise, that falls upon his ears? In a fast-moving world like ours, when the happenings in the remotest outlying parts are reported as quickly as though they were on our doorstep, and tomorrow's news becomes yesterday's history before you can say Jack Robinson, hundreds of names pass into our minds, and just as quickly pass out again. Names of vagabonds, dandies, lovers, ne'er-do-wells, heroes, tyrants, saints, historical names, names of men who changed the world—some of them household words, others just names that lurk in our subconscious. But who on earth were they?

We have mentioned Jack Robinson. But who on earth was Jack Robinson? He was a speedy fellow who did things so quickly that they were done before you could turn round—in fact, before you could say 'Jack Robinson'. He was undistinguished really, but his name has stuck. We hear old songs: 'Don't have any more, Mrs Moore ...', or poems, 'I do not love thee, Dr Fell ...'. But who on earth was Mrs Moore? And who on earth was Dr Fell? We have heard of the prophetess, Mother Shipton, the cruel Borgias (poisoners of the Renaissance), the kindly Lady with the Lamp, the foppish Beau Brummel, the exquisite Swedish Nightingale and the fickle Vicar of Bray. But who on earth were they?

The names could remain just names, and we would be none the wiser. In this book I have endeavoured to capture the people, and present them in a short biography. 'No great man lives in vain', wrote the historian, Thomas Carlyle. But no man or woman, great or otherwise, need live in vain. For we all have something to offer the eternal scheme of things that makes life interesting. If only someone can find that something.

All the characters in this book are real and have played their part, in a big or small way, to keep the wheels of the world turning. Hundreds more characters could be added to the list, but space permits but a select few. So I hope you will make your acquaintance now with people who before have been perhaps merely names. Interesting people, exciting people, people who deserve to live on in more than just name.

Some people have lived on unobtrusively by giving their name to a word which has taken over and obscured the person, such as Boycott, Hansom and Macintosh. These are known as eponyms, and they have not been forgotten in this book. They have been gathered together and appear in a selection as an epilogue.

Eileen Hellicar
Mitcham, 1981

Abelard

PETER ABELARD WAS AN eminent scholar, theologian and philosopher and one of the greatest thinkers of medieval times. But his popular claim to fame lies chiefly in his love affair with Héloïse.

He was born at Pallet, near Nantes, France, in 1079. After studying under two great diverse thinkers, Roscellinus, a nominalist, and William of Champeaux, a realist, he founded his own middle-of-the-road school of theology at Notre Dame in Paris. He was very popular as a teacher and, when he was thirty-six, he became tutor to Héloïse, the seventeen-year-old niece of Canon Fulbert of Notre Dame.

They fell in love and Abelard seduced Héloïse. He took her to Brittany and when their son was born he married her secretly with Fulbert's consent. But Héloïse denied the marriage and returned to her uncle as she did not want to hinder Abelard's career. Fulbert was furious at this decision. Believing it due to Abelard's connivance, he had Abelard castrated, so preventing him from preferment in holy orders (for only a 'whole' man could get preferment). Abelard then became a monk in the monastery of St Denis, and Héloïse became a nun in the convent at Argenteuil.

Abelard continued to teach, but his controversial theories angered the clergy. In 1121 he was condemned by a synod at Soissons for his teaching on the Trinity and sentenced to a period of confinement at Nogent-sur-Seine. But his pupils followed him and his hermitage soon became a monastic school named Le Paraclet. During this time Abelard wrote one of his most famous works, *Historia Calamitatum*, which described his ethical system. Heloïse was so moved by this that she wrote to him and so began their famous letters of love and suffering. Later Abelard was appointed Abbot of St Gildas-de-Rhuys in Brittany, and he bequeathed Le Paraclet to a sisterhood under Héloïse.

Still Abelard's teaching caused concern, and in 1142 his opponents, led by Bernard of Clairvaux, accused him of heresy. He was found guilty of this charge by a council at Sens and by the Pope. He set off for Rome to appeal personally to the Pope against the decision but died on the way at Cluny. He was buried at Le Paraclet. Héloïse died in 1164 and was laid at his side. In 1817 they were reburied in the Père Lachaise cemetery in Paris.

Al Capone

KNOWN AS SCARFACE, Al Capone was a notorious gangster and the leader of Chigago's underworld.

An Italian American, he was born in 1895 and joined the US Army as a machine-gunner in 1917. Two years later, when working as a barman, he joined a gang of thugs as strong-arm man in New York. He then moved to Chicago and became a gunman known as Scarface Al. When the Prohibition Act was passed in January 1920, he quickly rose to power as a bootlegger, controlling half the illegal liquor supplies in the United States. He ran gambling saloons and brothels in Chicago and organised the killing of rival gangs. Capone's gang was notorious for its ruthlessness in dealing with rivals. In the 'St Valentine's Day massacre' of 1929 they dressed as Chicago policemen and machine-gunned seven rival gang leaders. Capone was then left as supreme boss of Chicago's underworld.

His criminal dealings brought him in millions of pounds a year and during his infamous career he was responsible for more than 500 murders. In 1930 the FBI tried to convict him, but in vain as there was not enough evidence to bring him to justice. But in 1932 he was sent to Alcatraz prison for evading income tax. He was released in 1939 and went to live in Miami, Florida. Death came peacefully to Capone, not in the violent way he had inflicted it upon so many: he died in 1947 from pneumonia after a stroke.

Alcuin

ALCUIN WAS AN ANGLO-SAXON scholar and adviser to Charlemagne, King of the Franks (see p37). While in the service of Charlemagne, he helped to revive learning and culture in the barbarous pagan lands of western Europe.

He was born of a noble family in AD 735 and educated at the cathedral school at York under the care of Aelbert. In 776 Aelbert was made an Archbishop and Alcuin succeeded him as head of the school. In 781, while returning from a visit to Rome, he met Charlemagne at Parma. The Frankish king was very taken by his personality and learning and invited him to France to set up a school of learning at the royal court. The following year he accepted the invitation and took up residence at Charlemagne's palace at Aix-la-Chapelle. He devoted himself to teaching the royal family, including Charlemagne who often sat in at his lessons. Established as he was at the centre of the empire and enjoying the patronage of the great Emperor, he was in a unique position to influence the cultural future of Europe. He defended the orthodox teaching of Christianity against the current heresy of Adoptionism—that Christ was the adopted son of God.

Apart from two visits to England in 782 and 790, Alcuin stayed at the royal court until 796 when he left to take up the position of Abbot of the monastery at Tours. Under his care the monastery school soon became one of the most important in Charlemagne's empire. Whilst he was at Tours, Alcuin corresponded regularly with Charlemagne, writing over 200 letters to him and his friends in England.

He died in 804 in the knowledge that he had helped to return to the Continent Christian learning and culture, which until that time had been taught only in the English monasteries.

Amy Johnson

Amy Johnson, flew in an aeroplane
She flew to China and never came back again....

JUST BEFORE WORLD WAR II, children used to sing those lines to a speeded-up, staccato version of 'Daisy, Daisy, give me your answer do'. But little did they know that a few years later Amy Johnson would fly in an aeroplane, and never come back again.

Amy was the first woman to fly solo to Australia and the first woman to hold a British ground engineer's licence. She was born in Kingston-upon-Hull, Yorkshire, in 1903. When she was a child she persuaded her younger sister to accompany her on a five-shilling (25p) joy flight, and that was the beginning of her passion for flying. After graduating as a Bachelor of Arts at Sheffield University, she went to London to work as a solicitor's secretary. Towards the end of 1928 she joined the London Aeroplane Club and learned to fly at weekends and in the evenings. The following year, after 15¾ hours flying time, she obtained her pilot's licence, and later her engineer's licence.

She then decided to fly solo to Australia. For £600 she bought a second-hand de Havilland Moth. It was a biplane, 23ft 11in long, 8ft 9½in high, with a wing-span of 30ft and a speed of about 100mph. Amy had two extra fuel tanks fitted to the plane so that she could carry 60 gallons of petrol in addition to the 19 gallons carried in the usual tank. She tried to get financial backing for the flight, but nobody would take her seriously. She was not easily deterred and eventually her petrol supply was guaranteed by Lord Wakefield. Still the newspapers refused to help her in any way, believing that she would not be able to make the flight.

Amy was appalled by the lack of public interest and decided to make her own preparations. She had her Moth painted green and christened Jason. She learned how to use a parachute, and tied a spare propeller to the port side of the plane. Wearing a green flying suit and helmet, she took off from Croydon aerodrome just before 8am on the morning of Monday, 5 May 1930. She flew the 800-mile first lap of the journey to Vienna in 10 hours. She then flew another 800 miles to Constantinople in 12 hours. By now the world was beginning to take notice of the lone girl flyer, who had never been out of England before. The next day she flew 550 miles, over the Bosphorus and on to Asia Minor. During the next day, crossing the desert to Baghdad, she had to make a forced landing in a raging sandstorm. After 2 hours she took off again, and arrived in Baghdad on 8 May. On she went, over the Persian Gulf, on to Karachi, Calcutta, Rangoon and Bangkok. On the thirteenth day she flew down the Malay peninsula to Singapore. She was battling with treacherous weather, but still she flew on, heading over the East Indies making for the Timor Sea and the last stage of the journey to Port Darwin. By night-time on the seventeenth day of her flight all contact with her was lost. A full-scale search was just about to be launched when news came through that she had landed safely at Haliloelik, a little village in the East Indies, that had no telephone. It was not until morning, when Amy could send a telegram, that the world knew she was safe. People tried to dissuade her from continuing her flight, but she was adamant. She pressed on, over the dangerous Timor Sea, and reached Port Darwin at 3pm on her nineteenth day out of England. She had flown 12,000 miles, averaging just over 600 miles a day.

The world was astonished and delighted. The *Daily Mail* presented her with a cheque for £10,000 and she was awarded a CBE by the King. Two years later she married another pilot, James Mollison, but the marriage ended in divorce in 1938. She had no children. In 1932 she made another solo flight—this time to the Cape, breaking the time record that was held by her husband.

In 1939, at the start of World War II, she joined the Air Transport Auxiliary, and was lost over the Thames Estuary on 5 January 1941 while piloting a plane for the Air Ministry.

Annie Oakley

KNOWN AS LITTLE SURE SHOT, Annie Oakley was the greatest woman rifle shot the world has ever known.

She was born on 13 August 1860, in a log cabin in Darke County, Ohio, and her real name was Phoebe Anne Oakley Moses. By the time she was six years old she was using a rifle to help hunt food for the family. Her aim was spectacular and she became one of the best-known hunters in the country. While still in her teens she won a shooting match in Cincinatti against the crack marksman, Frank Butler. Annie then became internationally famous and later she and Butler were married. As Butler and Oakley they toured the States in circuses and music hall acts until 1885 when they joined Buffalo Bill's Wild West Show (see p29). Annie's performances were so startling and her audiences so great that she was given top billing as 'Miss Annie Oakley, the Peerless Lady Wing-Shot'. Annie Oakley was a name she chose for herself. Her husband now acted as her manager and assistant.

Annie just could not miss. Her aim succeeded every time. From 30 yards she could hit a coin tossed in the air, the edge of a playing card, and the end of a cigarette held in Butler's lips. Her acts were breathtakingly riveting. Once when she was touring in Berlin, she shot a cigarette from the lips of Kaiser Wilhelm.

In 1901 Annie was seriously injured in a train crash, but fortunately recovered sufficiently to carry on performing. She and Butler then continued to tour giving shooting lessons and demonstrations.

Annie Oakley died on 3 November 1926 but her name lives on, not only as a crack shot, but also in the United States to denote a complimentary ticket. The hole which is punched in such a ticket is reminiscent of the hole Annie fired into playing cards during her performances, and so any free ticket is known as an Annie Oakley.

Attila the Hun

KNOWN THROUGHOUT EUROPE AS the 'Scourge of God', Attila, one of the greatest of the barbarian rulers, was King of the Huns, a nomadic Asiatic people, from about AD 433 until his death in 453.

Not much is known about his early life, except that he was born about 406 and was the son of Mundzuk, a member of the ruling Hun family. As a young man he was sent to Rome as a hostage for the good behaviour of his tribe and there he became a relentless enemy of the city. When he was twenty-seven he succeeded his uncle, Ruas, as ruler. At first his brother Bleda shared the power with him, but in 444 Attila murdered Bleda and became sole king. Under Ruas's rule the Huns had spread from the Caspian steppes and had reached the River Danube in repeated invasions against the Eastern Roman Empire. Attila, ruthlessly ambitious, made large-scale invasions and devastated the whole area between the Black Sea and the Mediterranean. He defeated the Byzantine emperor Theodosius II and forced him to pay huge protection payments. He then pressed on through Gaul, demanding half the Western Roman Empire, and at Châlons-sur-Marne suffered his only defeat, by Roman and Visigothic troops, in one of the cruellest battles in history. The following year, 452, he devastated northern Italy and advanced upon Rome, but left hastily after being subdued by a personal visit from Pope Leo I. Attila was planning a second invasion of Italy in 453, when he died suddenly from a haemorrhage on the night of his marriage to Ildico. After his death his empire collapsed.

As the old adage says, it is an ill wind that blows nobody any good. And one pleasant result of Attila's ravaging of northern Italy was that some of the conquered people took refuge among the islands and lagoons of the Adriatic and founded a community which eventually grew into the city of Venice.

Beau Brummell

BEAU BRUMMELL was an English dandy and a leader of fashion in the eighteenth century. He was responsible for introducing stiffening into men's cravats—a fashion that caused such a sensation that other dandies were consumed with envy.

His real name was George Bryan Brummell and he was the son of William Brummell, private secretary to the Prime Minister, Lord North. Although he was not highborn, the Eton and Oxford educated Brummell was an intimate friend of George IV when he was Prince Regent and was the arbiter of Regency taste in dress and manners.

When he came into the fortune left him by his father, he settled in an elegant house in Chesterfield Street in London's Mayfair, and soon gained his reputation as a socialite, wit and dandy. He dressed with impeccable care in perfect clothes. Dressing was an art to him, and it is said that the Prince Regent often went to his house to watch him dress, hoping to learn the art.

The Prince Regent much enjoyed Brummell's company. He liked the way he mixed his snuff and admired the way he stiffened his cravat. Then their friendship declined over Brummell's rudeness to Mrs Fitzherbert, the lady with whom the Prince was in love. But Brummell was not to be put down. In July 1813 he was invited to a 'Dandy Ball' given by Lord Alvanley, at which the Prince Regent was guest of honour. When the Prince saw Brummell arrive he snubbed him, but Brummell knew how to get back at the Prince, and asked in a loud voice 'Alvanley, who's your fat friend?' That was the end of his association with the future King.

Sadly, like many young socialites in those days, Beau Brummell gambled heavily. Eventually, his gambling debts caught up with him and on 16 May 1816 he made a hurried departure to Calais. He spent the rest of his life in France. In September 1830 he was appointed British Consul in Caen, but two years later he asked to be released from this sinecure. In May 1835 he was sent to prison for eight weeks. The experience broke his spirit and in 1837 he began to show signs of mental deterioration. He neglected his health and appearance until eventually he was taken into the asylum of the Good Saviour in Caen, where he died on 30 March 1840.

Beau Nash

THE AUTHOR, OLIVER GOLDSMITH, described his friend Beau Nash as having 'too much merit not to become remarkable, but too much folly to arrive at greatness'. Nash certainly was remarkable and is remembered in history as the 'uncrowned King of Bath'.

Richard Nash, to give him his proper name, was born in Swansea in 1674 and was the son of a glass-maker. After leaving Oxford without taking a degree, he spent a short time in the Army and then became a lawyer at London's Inner Temple. But his first love was gambling and in 1705 he went to the decaying health resort of Bath. There he became assistant to the master of ceremonies, Captain Webster, and when Webster was killed in a duel over gambling at cards, Nash took over his job and began a forty-year reign that transformed Bath into a fashionable health resort unequalled in England.

He began by dressing the part of 'king'. He wore a coat decorated with braid and lace, an embroidered waistcoat and ruffled shirt, and instead of the usual white wig, he chose a black one, topped by a bejewelled cream-coloured hat, which he wore at a rakish angle. This foppishness soon earned him his nickname of Beau. But Nash was no mere fop. He soon set to work to improve the conditions in Bath. He improved the lighting and cleanliness of the streets, had new roads built, suppressed duelling, reformed dress and drove beggars and thieves from the city. He initiated the building of the Pump Room and the Assembly Rooms and encouraged rich businessmen to put up other new buildings. He laid down a pattern of daily living for visitors which had to be strictly adhered to, always beginning with three glasses of warm water in the Pump Room.

Very soon Bath grew prosperous and elegant and all the outstanding personalities of the day flocked to take its waters, gossip in its Pump Room and gamble at its tables. But whoever they were, royalty or commoner, they were ruled by Nash. He was King of Bath, and he drove round its streets in a chariot drawn by six greys and driven by lace-clad lackeys blowing French horns.

Nash died in 1761, aged eighty-seven, and his memorial is in Bath Abbey, where the city he ruled for so long gave him a lavish funeral.

The Black Prince

Brave Gaunt, thy father and myself
Rescued the Black Prince, that young Mars of men,
From the ranks of many thousand French.

IT IS NOT REALLY known why the Black Prince was so named. Some
say it was because of the colour of his armour, but Jean Froissart, the
fourteenth-century historian, wrote in his *Chronicles* that he was
'styled black by terror of his arms'. One thing is certain—he was not
known as the Black Prince during his lifetime. The first recorded use
of the nickname was in 1569.

His real name was Prince Edward of Woodstock and he was the
eldest son of Edward III and Queen Philippa, and brother of John of
Gaunt. He was the third heir to the throne to be created Prince of
Wales, but he never became King as he died while his father was still
on the throne.

Prince Edward was born in 1330, eight years before the Hundred
Years War began. He was created Earl of Chester when he was three,
Duke of Cornwall when he was seven, and Prince of Wales at thirteen.
By the time he was sixteen, he had won his spurs at the Battle of Crécy
where he had commanded the right wing. During this battle, the King
of Bohemia, who had fought against the English, was killed. On his
shield were his crest of three white feathers and his motto, *Ich Dien*—
I serve. The Black Prince took both the device and the motto for
himself and these have been used by Princes of Wales ever since.

The Black Prince was a brilliant and chivalrous soldier. He fought
in many battles against the French, including the Battle of Poitiers,
where he captured King John of France and brought him back to
England. But he did not die on the battlefield. It was the Black Plague
that killed him in 1376 at the age of forty-six. He is buried in Canterbury Cathedral with his helmet and gauntlets above his tomb.

In 1361 the Black Prince married his cousin, Joan, known as the Fair
Maid of Kent. They had two sons. The elder died before the Black
Prince and the younger, Richard, became king as Richard II when the
Black Prince's father, Edward III, died in 1377.

Blondin

EVERY SO OFTEN LIFE produces a wonder man, and that title for the nineteenth century must surely go to Charles Blondin, one of the most daring acrobats of all time, who owed his fame and fortune to his feat of crossing Niagara Falls on a tightrope.

Blondin's real name was Jean-François Gravelet and he was born in St Omer, France, on 28 February 1824. When he was five years old, his parents sent him to train as an acrobat at the School of Gymnastics at Lyons. After only six months' training, he made his first public appearance and soon won acclaim for his nerve-racking, daring performances and became known as 'The Little Wonder'.

In 1859 he made the first of his many hazardous tightrope walks across Niagara Falls. The tightrope was 1,100ft long and 160ft above the rapidly swirling water. Blondin took 20 minutes to cross—an average of 55ft a minute. When he reached the middle of the crossing he stopped and let down a rope to a ship waiting below in case he fell. The ship's crew tied a glass and bottle of drink to the end of the rope. Blondin hauled it up, poured a drink and balancing on one leg, toasted the terrified crowds watching his performance.

After that feat Blondin made a number of crossings, always with a different theatrical variation. He crossed blindfold, trundling a man in a wheelbarrow, carrying a man on his back, on stilts, with his legs in a sack, twirling an umbrella, and once he sat down midway to cook and eat an omelette. Blondin made a fortune from this tightrope act and soon after his last performance he settled in England. In 1861 he appeared at Crystal Palace in London where he turned somersaults on stilts on a tightrope 170ft above the ground. He even walked across a rope, stretched between the masts of a ship, in a violent thunderstorm. Nothing seemed to frighten him and he continued to perform until he was over seventy. His last act was at Belfast in 1896. He died the following year, at Ealing in west London, nine days before his seventy-third birthday.

Bloody Mary

Still amorous, and fond, and billing,
Like Philip and Mary on a shilling.

THE WOMAN who earned herself the title of Bloody Mary was Mary I, daughter of Henry VIII and his first wife, Catherine of Aragon.

Mary was born in 1516 and was brought up as a devout Catholic by her Spanish mother. She was a lively, intelligent child until she was about ten. Then Henry took her away from her mother, whom he intended to divorce since she could not produce the son and heir he so desperately wanted, and never allowed them to see each other again. That in itself was bad enough for Mary, but when Henry, who had renounced his Catholic faith, married his second wife, Anne Boleyn, Mary was declared illegitimate and denied the right to succeed to the throne. Mary spent the following years in bitterness and isolation.

Henry died in 1547 and was succeeded by Edward VI, his nine-year-old-son by Jane Seymour. But Edward was a sickly child and reigned for only six years. Before he died his advisers, fearing he would be succeeded by his Catholic elder sister, Mary, persuaded him to name Lady Jane Grey as his successor. Lady Jane reigned for just nine days and Mary at last became queen in 1553. The country seemed pleased at her accession and Mary took their welcome as support for her determination to restore the Catholic religion to England and to get rid of all heresy. The Church of England was suppressed by Parliament and the Mass was restored. But Protestantism persisted and Mary launched her reign of terror that was to earn her the nickname 'Bloody Mary'. In four years more than 300 people were burned at the stake, among them Thomas Cranmer, Archbishop of Canterbury, Nicholas Ridley, Bishop of London, and Bishop Hugh Latimer.

Mary's reign was not a happy one, for her or the country. England was dismayed at her choice of a husband, Philip II, king of unfriendly Spain, whom she married in 1554. The prospect of a succession of Catholic children on the throne and England becoming a Spanish dependency was a real fear, and a small rebellion, led by Sir Thomas Wyatt, to try to prevent the wedding, broke out in Kent. Sadly Mary's marriage was not a happy one. She adored Philip, but he spent little time with her. He dragged England into Spain's war with France, and Calais, which England had held for more than 200 years, was lost. The country was growing more and more rebellious against their fanatical queen. Spanish at heart, she had never really understood the English, and plots were now afoot to replace her with her half-sister Elizabeth, Henry's daughter by Anne Boleyn. But nature took its course and Mary, who had never managed to produce the child she so much wanted, died in 1558 at the age of forty-two. She is remembered as the most unpleasant and unpopular queen in British history.

Bonnie Prince Charlie

Speed bonnie boat, like a bird on the wing,
Onward the sailors cry;
Carry the lad who is born to be king
Over the sea to Skye.

THE LAD WHO WAS 'born to be king', but in fact never became king, was Charles Edward Philip Casimir Stuart, who lives on in history as 'Bonnie Prince Charlie', or the 'Young Pretender'.

The legend of Bonnie Prince Charlie began in June 1745 when he led the Second Jacobite Rebellion in an attempt to regain the British throne from the Hanoverian George II and restore his own father, James Stuart, as king.

Bonnie Prince Charlie, grandson of the deposed James II and the eldest son of James Francis Edward Stuart, the Old Pretender, was born in Rome in 1720 and brought up as a Catholic. In 1744 he was invited to Paris by the French Government, who were planning an expedition to Britain to oust the Protestant George II and re-establish Catholic Stuart rule in England and Scotland. A storm prevented the expedition from getting under way, and Bonnie Prince Charlie set out independently with seven friends. He landed at Moidart, Inverness-shire, in June 1745 and he soon had more than 1,000 Highlanders rallying to his cause. Two months later, on 19 August, his wild, undisciplined following had grown to more than 2,000 and he raised his standard at Glenfinnan. With each day his army increased and he marched through Perth, crossed the River Forth, captured Edinburgh and on 21 September, defeated Sir John Cope and his government forces at the Battle of Prestonpans.

On 1 November, after spending six weeks consolidating his army in Edinburgh, he marched into England. Initially he was very successful. He captured Carlisle and by 4 December, had pressed on as far as Derby, 127 miles from London. The English Government was thrown into panic, and the royal yacht was at the ready to take George II to Hanover. Then, on 6 December, the Prince's commanders saw that the 5,000 Highlanders were outnumbered by the king's 30,000 men under the command of the king's son, the Duke of Cumberland, and they forced Bonnie Prince Charlie to retreat. He headed back to Scotland. Carlisle was recaptured by Cumberland, but the Jacobites gained one more victory, at Falkirk on 17 January 1746. Cumberland's army pushed them north, and the Jacobites were finally annihilated at the Battle of Culloden on 16 April. Cumberland's army had slaughtered 1,200 half-starved and exhausted clansmen.

Bonnie Prince Charlie escaped the massacre and for the next five months Cumberland, who had earned the nickname of the 'Butcher', hunted him among the Highlands and islands of Scotland. A price of £30,000 was put on Bonnie Prince Charlie's head, but no one betrayed him. Loyal clansmen and women risked their lives to hide him and eventually Flora Macdonald disguised him as her maid and took the fugitive prince by boat 'over the sea to Skye'. On 29 September, he left Scotland for Brittany, where he was given hospitality by the French king. For the next twenty years he wandered round Europe bitter in defeat and living a life of drunkenness and debauchery until he finally settled in Italy. He never gave up the hope of a Stuart restoration, and when he reached Rome he assumed the title of Charles III of Great Britain. The Pope refused to recognise his claim and Bonnie Prince Charlie retired to Florence, where he lived for many years before returning to Rome. His wife, Princess Louise of Stolberg, whom he had married in 1772, left him after six years of marriage and went to live in a convent. In 1784 Charlie sent for Charlotte, his natural daughter by his mistress, Clementina Walkinshaw, and she devotedly tended him until his death in 1788.

Buddha

BUDDHA, MEANING THE AWAKENED ONE, was the title taken by Siddhartha Gautama, founder of the Buddhist faith.

Buddha was born in Kapilavastu, near Nepal in northern India, about 563 BC. He was born into a noble family and brought up in luxury. At the age of sixteen he married a princess named Yasodhara, and they had one son. Being the son of a high-caste warrior, Buddha knew nothing of the unpleasant and difficult side of life until one day, when he was twenty-nine, he was out riding with his charioteer and he saw three things which awakened him—first an old man, then an ill man and finally a dead man. He then realised that there was suffering in the world and that life had an end, and he determined to give up his comfortable life and seek spiritual truth.

Leaving his wife and child behind he became an ascetic, denying himself all pleasures. Accompanied by five other ascetics he wandered over northern India for nearly six years. In the end he almost faded away with weakness and then realised that ascetism was futile and was not the answer. So he turned to what he called the 'Middle Way', of meditation and spiritual exercise. Meditating cross-legged one day beneath a pipal tree—the sacred Bodhi (Bo) tree—about 528 BC, Buddha experienced complete enlightenment. He had realised the cause of suffering and the way to overcome it. He knew then that he was the 'Awakened One'. He took to preaching, and gave his first sermon at Sarnath, near Benares, and this sermon became the basis of the Buddhist faith. His mission was to preach the Four Noble Truths: suffering itself; the cause of suffering; the ceasing of suffering; and freedom from suffering. Buddha believed that all life was suffering because man craved for permanence and self identity, and that only when this craving was eliminated could suffering cease. The state of awareness which Buddha achieved is known as Nirvana, and is the ultimate goal of the Buddhist faith. This salvation is achieved through an 'Eightfold Path'—eight stages of behaviour beginning with belief and working up to contemplation.

Buddha continued to wander and preach for forty-three years. He returned briefly to his home town and converted his wife, father and other members of his family to his faith. He died in 483 BC in the arms of Ananda, one of his disciples, at Kusinagara, near Nepal, from dysentery after eating contaminated pork. He was aged eighty and his last words to his disciples were 'Behold now, brethren, decay is inherent in all component things. Work out your salvation with diligence. Be a light unto yourselves, for there is no other light.' His body was cremated and his ashes distributed to followers who scattered them beneath burial mounds.

Although Siddhartha Gautama was the original Buddha, Buddhist tradition holds that other Buddhas have appeared from time to time throughout history, and will appear in future whenever they are needed by mankind.

Buffalo Bill

THE NICKNAME, BUFFALO BILL, was given to the American William Frederick Cody when he provided buffalo meat for the labourers building the Kansas Pacific Railway in 1876-8. In eighteen months he is said to have killed 4,280 buffaloes.

Cody, an army scout, showman and buffalo hunter, was born in Scott County, Iowa, on 26 February 1846. He had only about one year's schooling, and when he was eleven he took his first job as a wagon messenger with a freight company. After that he served on a wagon train and later took part in his first trapping expedition. When he was still only fourteen, he became a pony express rider and completed one of the longest rides in history, covering more than 320 miles at an average speed of 15 miles an hour. During the American Civil War he scouted for the 9th Kansas Cavalry against the Indians and later on, while serving in the 5th Cavalry, he killed Yellowhand, the Cheyenne chief, single handed. He then began hunting buffalo to feed the railway builders.

For a while he went on the stage and starred in a revue *The Scouts of the Prairie*, written by a friend, Ned Buntline. In 1883 he gave up the stage to organise his Wild West Show, which was to become known as 'Buffalo Bill's Wild West Show'. The show, which contained Indians, cowboys, rough-riders and sharp-shooters, was immensely successful and toured extensively in America and Europe. Eventually the extravagant show got into financial difficulties and Cody combined it with 'Pawnee Bill's Great Far East Show'. In 1913, Cody lost his shares in the show and took to performing in other people's shows and writing Wild West novels. He retained his zest for life and his riding skill until he died at Denver, Colorado, on 10 January 1917, aged almost seventy-one.

Caedmon

CALLED 'THE FATHER OF ENGLISH SONG', Caedmon, who lived in Northumberland in the seventh century AD, was the first English Christian
poet. All that is known about him comes from the Venerable Bede's
Ecclesiastical History of the English People (see p148).

Caedmon, an uneducated, ignorant herdsman, ashamedly left the
company he was keeping one night because he could not comply with
the request that every guest should sing. He went sadly to bed and
dreamed that an angel appeared and commanded him to sing the
Creation, which he did, uttering verses he had never heard before.
When he awoke he remembered every word of his dream and related
it to the bailiff at the farm where he worked. The astounded bailiff
took him to the monastery at Whitby, called at that time, Streanes-
shalch, and to the monks' surprise, he again sang what is now known
as *Caedmon's Hymn*. The Abbess, St Hilda, believed that he was
divinely inspired, and to make sure, Caedmon was asked to compose
more verses of sacred history which the monks first explained to him
since he was illiterate and could not read them for himself. By morning
he had completed the task and the monks believed that they had
witnessed a miracle. Caedmon was then invited to join the monastery.

During the rest of his life as a monk, Caedmon produced poetry
from scriptures expounded to him by his more learned brethren. He
wrote only sacred poetry and his one aim was to turn man from sin to
righteous living. Of all the poetry that Caedmon wrote, only his dream
Hymn remains as his authentic work, and this is in the Bodleian
Library in Oxford. Illiterate though he was, Caedmon's dream *Hymn*
influenced much later Anglo-Saxon poetry.

Calamity Jane

THE NAME CALAMITY JANE has come to mean one who always predicts misfortune, or takes a pessimistic view of life. But the real Calamity Jane, a frontierswoman of the American West, was not at all like that and how she came to be so nicknamed is not really known. One possible explanation is that the gun she always carried symbolised calamity to philandering males.

Martha Jane Burke, to give her her real name, was born about 1852 in Princeton, Montana, but moved with her parents to Virginia City when she was about twelve. She frequented the mining towns of the area, and soon became well-known for her prowess with a gun and as a horsewoman. Flaunting convention, she wore men's clothes and went on wild drinking sprees. During her colourful career, she earned a reputation for bravery and apparently served as a scout with the Indian fighters, General Custer and General Miles.

For a while she was a prostitute in various frontier towns, mostly around Deadwood, South Dakota. In the 1890s she appeared in Wild West shows, and later she became a pony express rider carrying the mail between Deadwood and Custer, Montana. In 1901 she appeared at the Buffalo Pan American Exposition.

In 1884 she became the heroine of Edward Wheeler's series of cheap novels. In fiction she is portrayed as the beautiful, buckskin-clad sweetheart of Deadwood Dick, fighting for justice against the baddies in the Black Hills of Dakota. She died in 1903 aged about fifty-one.

Capability Brown

The omnipotent Magician Brown appears,
He speaks; the lawn in front becomes a lake;
Woods vanish, hills subside and valleys rise....

THE OMNIPOTENT MAGICIAN TO whom the poet William Cowper is referring is Lancelot Brown, one of the greatest landscape gardeners of the eighteenth century. He earned his nickname, Capability Brown, because he always assured his prospective employers that their land had 'great capabilities'.

Brown, who was born in 1716, became a gardener at Stowe, Lord Cobham's estate in Buckinghamshire. In 1741, Lord Cobham made him head gardener and by the time Lord Temple inherited the estate from his uncle in 1749, Stowe was one of the finest landscaped estates in Britain.

Capability Brown stayed at Stowe until 1751, when he left to set up his own business as architect and landscape gardener. He was patronised by most of the landed gentry and he transformed more than 100 gardens. Brown's idea was to do away with formal gardens, and create vistas and natural settings, so surrounding his clients' houses with parkland and pastoral beauty.

Among the gardens he landscaped are Blenheim in Oxfordshire, Harewood in Yorkshire and Bowood in Wiltshire. Brown died in 1783, aged sixty-seven.

Casanova

THE NAME CASANOVA USUALLY conjures up pictures of a male flirt. But the real Casanova was more than that. He was an adventurer, a gambler and a charlatan as well.

Giovanni Jacopo Casanova was born in Venice in 1725. By the time he was twenty-one he had been expelled from a seminary for immoral conduct, worked as a secretary to a cardinal, served as a soldier in the Venetian service, and played the violin in an orchestra. He then began his notorious career, wandering through the capitals of Europe posing as a preacher, chemist, diplomat, and many other fancies that came into his mind, mixing with high society wherever he went.

In 1755 he was imprisoned in Venice for practising magic and masonry. He made a daring escape from prison and fled to Paris, where he became director of the state lottery and came into contact with leading lights such as Louis XV and Madame de Pompadour. But Casanova did not stay long. As always happened he left in disgrace because of his amorous adventures. He visited almost every court in Europe, winning favour and then disappearing. He made a fortune and lost it gambling. He was made a knight of the papal order of the Golden Spur, and on a diplomatic mission to Holland he was given the title of Chevalier de Seingalt.

Casanova ended up by becoming, in 1785, secretary and librarian to Count Waldstein at the castle of Dux in Bohemia. This time he did not have to move on, but stayed with the count for thirteen years until his death in 1798. While he was at the castle he wrote his famous *Memoirs*, which give an excellent account of life in the eighteenth century.

Cesare Borgia

IF EVER THERE WAS a villain, it was Cesare Borgia. He was a member of an infamous Spanish family that rose to prominence in Italy during the fifteenth and sixteenth centuries.

When Alfonso of Aragon conquered Naples in 1443, Alonso Borgia, who was Bishop of Valencia, went to Italy with him, and rose to high office in his service. Alonso became Pope, as Calixtus III, in April 1455, and conferred high offices of church and state upon his many relations, especially his nephew, Rodrigo, who became Pope Alexander VI in August 1492. Rodrigo was unscrupulous and fathered many illegitimate children, among whom was Cesare, born of Vanozza dei Catanei in 1475.

Cesare was his father's favourite son, and he used Rodrigo's power to help him in his evil doings. In 1492 he became Bishop of Valencia and in the following year he was made a cardinal. In 1498 Cesare was released from his office of cardinal after it became publicly known that he was the illegitimate son of the Pope. He then became a papal ambassador and set out for France with a dispensation enabling the divorced Louis XII to marry Anne of Brittany. The grateful French king presented him with the Dukedom of Valentinois, 'a fine city on the Rhône, bringing in a Revenue of 10,000 scudi a year', and promised him support in his plan to conquer central Italy to carve out a principality for himself.

Cesare married Charlotte d'Albret, sister of the King of Navarre, and returned to Italy where he became known as Il Valentino. He then became standard bearer and captain general of the Church. Using all his murderous skill and cunning, in three campaigns from 1499 to 1502, he conquered the principal cities of Romagna and Bologna, leaving a trail of carnage in his wake. Anyone who hindered him was murdered, usually by poisoning. Tuscany was his next goal, but his vile, meteoric career was cut short by the death of his father in August 1503.

Cesare was now at the mercy of his enemies—and they were legion—but serious illness prevented him from dealing with the crisis. Then the arch-enemy of the Borgias, Giuliano della Rovere, was elected Pope as Julius II in October 1503. Cesare was forced to leave Italy under guard and imprisoned in a fortress in Spain. After two years he escaped to join the army of his brother-in-law, the King of Navarre. He died fighting in the invasion of Castile in March 1507.

Cesare Borgia, who left behind a legend of tyranny, poisoning, wild orgies, murder and greed, was the subject of Machiavelli's political treatise *The Prince* (see p96).

Charlemagne

CHARLEMAGNE, MEANING CHARLES THE GREAT, was King of the Franks and the first Holy Roman Emperor. He waged religious war throughout Europe in an attempt to combat paganism.

Charles was the son of the Frankish king, Pepin the Short. When Pepin died in 768, Charles and his brother Carloman jointly inherited the crown. Three years later Carloman died and Charles became sole king. In the forty-six years of his reign he united the pagan kingdoms of western Europe into a vast Christian empire extending from the Baltic to the Mediterranean.

In building his empire, Charlemagne led fifty-three military expeditions against northern Italy, northern Spain, France and Germany. In the year 799 he saved Pope Leo III from deposition and the following year, the Pope rewarded him by crowning him first Emperor of the Holy Roman Empire.

Charlemagne was an intelligent man and could speak Latin, Greek, and German. But he could not read or write. He was a first-class administrator and in an attempt to revive learning and culture, he established schools under the governorship of Alcuin, whom he imported from York (see p11). Charlemagne was as successful in governing his great Christian empire as he had been ruthless in creating it.

Charlemagne, who was said to be 8ft tall and as strong as an ox, had been married eight times and had fourteen children. He died in 814 and is buried at Aix-la-Chapelle. Like all great historical characters Charlemagne is as much a part of legend as reality, and his adventures and those of his palladins (knights) are told in the Carolingian legends.

Davy Crockett

Davy, Davy Crockett
King of the Wild frontier.

THE HERO OF MANY American folk tales, Davy Crockett was a frontiersman, soldier and politician. He was born in Tennessee in 1786. During the Creek War of 1813-14 he served as a scout under Andrew Jackson, and after the war he became a Justice of the Peace in Tennessee. His judgement as a JP was based on what he called 'natural born sense instead of law learning', and he proudly boasted that none of his decisions was ever reversed. Somebody suggested to him in fun that he should run for Congress. So he did, and he was elected for three terms—1827-9, 1829-31, 1833-5, becoming known as the 'coonskin Congressman' because of his love of hunting. He was a prodigious hunter of bears and claims to have killed more than a hundred in nine months.

He lost his seat as a Congressman because of his opposition to the policies of President Jackson and then decided to go to Texas to defend the Alamo, a fortified mission in San Antonio. During the Texas rebellion against Mexico in 1836, the Texan army under William B. Travis was besieged at the Alamo by the Mexican army. After a thirteen-day bombardment, the Mexicans gained entrance and every Texan defender—187 of them—was killed in hand-to-hand combat, Davy Crockett among them.

Almost immediately after he was killed he was made into a folk hero who was fearless and capable of anything.

The Desert Fox

THE DESERT FOX WAS the nickname given to Field-Marshal Erwin Rommel, Commander of the German Afrika Korps during World War II, because of his bold, unorthodox tactics.

Rommel, who was born in 1891, fought in World War I and gained an award for merit. Later he joined the German National Socialist Party and became a member of Hitler's bodyguard (see p58). He fought in the 1939 Polish campaign at the beginning of World War II, and in 1940 brilliantly commanded an armoured division in France. Hitler then appointed him commander of the Afrika Korps to reinforce the Italians in Libya. He was an immediate success and inflicted many reverses on the British 8th Army. In November 1942 he was beaten at the Battle of El Alamein, 80 miles west of Alexandria, by Britain's Field Marshal Montgomery and his troops. The British pushed him right back across Africa to Tunisia. His final strike against the 8th Army at Medinine failed and Rommel returned to Germany, a sick man, leaving the Axis army doomed to destruction.

In 1944, when the allies landed in Normandy, Rommel became commander of the anti-invasion forces defending the Low Countries and northern France, and was wounded on 17 July. Three days later, on 20 July, he took part in the plot to assassinate Hitler. The plot was blown and Rommel was given the option of being court-martialled and shot or of committing suicide. He died the following October, presumably by his own hand.

As a fighting soldier Rommel was a genius and exercised great personal influence over his troops, yet he seemed to have no idea of the administrative side of warfare. He was bold and incredibly daring, but his health was not always as strong as he would have liked and his nerve was apt to crack suddenly. But nevertheless as a commander of a small mobile army, the Desert Fox had few equals in modern times.

Dick Turpin

And the fame of Dick Turpin had been something less
If he'd ne'er rode to York on his bonnie Black Bess.

KNOWN AS THE 'King of the Road', Dick Turpin was a highwayman who, according to legend, rode his horse, Black Bess, non-stop from London to York (nearly 200 miles) to avoid capture.

Dick was born in 1705 at the Bell Inn, Hempstead, Essex, where his father was the innkeeper. When he was sixteen he was apprenticed to a butcher at Whitechapel in London's East End. To supplement his earnings he became a footpad—and so began his infamous career.

After his marriage in 1728 he started his own business as a butcher in Essex, but was accused of stocking his shop with the carcasses of stolen cattle and sheep. He then joined Gregory's Gang in Epping Forest and became an expert smuggler, housebreaker and sheep stealer. In 1735 this gang broke up and Dick became a highwayman, working mostly around south London. The following year he began his famous partnership with Tom King and the pair won fame as highwaymen in Epping Forest and Hounslow Heath.

This partnership lasted for just one year, for Dick Turpin accidentally shot King dead while firing at a policeman during a fight in London. Turpin then mounted Black Bess and fled—supposedly non-stop to Yorkshire. There he assumed the name of John Palmer and started to trade in stolen horses.

Early in 1739 he was arrested for horse stealing. Fearing that the police might discover who their prisoner really was, he wrote to his brother in Essex and asked him to send someone to York to swear that he was John Palmer. But unfortunately for Turpin, the postmaster at Essex was his old schoolmaster and he recognised Turpin's handwriting. He opened the letter and hastened to York to expose the true identity of the horse stealer—and was rewarded with £200 from the authorities for doing so.

On the morning of 7 April 1739, Turpin was hanged on what is now York Racecourse. According to one contemporary report the crowd were so distressed at the hanging of such a famous character that they stole his body and buried it in quicklime.

The cell where he was kept before his execution is in York Castle Museum.

Dick Whittington

Turn again, Whittington, thou worthy citizen
Lord Mayor of London.

DICK WHITTINGTON IS CHIEFLY remembered for his cat. But the panto-mime story about the poor boy who made his way to London when he heard that the streets were paved with gold, enchanting though it is, bears little resemblance to the truth.

Dick, who was born about 1358, was certainly not a pauper. He was the youngest son of Sir William Whittington of Pauntley in Glouces-tershire. When he was about thirteen he went to London to be ap-prenticed to Sir Ivo Fitzwaryn, a mercer and Merchant Adventurer, who was a distant relation of Dick's mother. Dick was a keen appren-tice and within twenty years was the richest merchant of his day. Not only was he successful himself, but he married his master's daughter, Alice Fitzwaryn, heiress to her father's fortune. He was a kind, chari-table man and a great benefactor to the City of London. He lent vast sums of money to Richard II, Henry IV and Henry V, and when Henry IV's daughters were married Dick bought their wedding dresses for them. He also founded a college, named after himself, to maintain priests to pray for the warring 'cousin kings', Richard II and Henry IV, at the start of the Wars of the Roses.

Dick's benefactions to London—almshouses, endowments to librar-ies and the restoration of St Bartholomew's Hospital—were rewarded. He achieved the highest honour by becoming Lord Mayor of London three times, 1397-8, 1406-7 and 1419-20. In 1398, 1407 and 1420 he was Master of the Mercers, the richest of the City of London compan-ies. In 1416 he became Member of Parliament for London.

Dick died in 1423 at the age of sixty-five. He had no children and his fortune was left to charity and for public purposes such as the rebuild-ing of Newgate Prison. His tomb, which he had built for himself in St Michael's Church, Paternoster Royal, was destroyed in the Great Fire of London, 1666.

Many legends have grown around Dick Whittington, among them the story of how when he was entertaining Henry V and Queen Catherine he burned not only expensive cedar logs to keep them warm, but £60,000 worth of bonds as well. The pantomime story of Dick and his cat first appeared in a ballad in 1605. Various explanations have been given for the cat appearing in the story, but the most likely seems to be that Dick traded in coal which was brought to London in a cat (the old name for a coal- and timber-carrying sailing vessel used in the north-east of England).

On Highgate Hill, in north London, a stone marks the spot where Dick heard the City's Bow Bells pealing out their plea: 'Turn again, Whittington, thou worthy citizen.'

Dr Crippen

DR CRIPPEN WAS A murderer, but he is remembered for the way he was caught, rather than for the crime he committed: he was the first criminal to be trapped by wireless telegraphy.

Hawley Harvey Crippen was born in Michigan, USA, in 1861. He qualified as a doctor of homeopathy but then became an agent for a patent medicine company known as Professor Munyon's Remedies. In 1897 he came to England to open the British branch of the company. His second wife, Cora Mackamotzki, a struggling opera singer known professionally as Belle Elmore, accompanied him, and they lived at 39 Hilldrop Crescent, Holloway, London. Belle was not successful as an opera singer so, determined to be on the stage, she tried to become a music-hall artiste. She played up to any man she thought could help her to become successful and Crippen uncomplainingly paid out for her expensive fineries. He neglected his work and was sacked from Munyon's Remedies in 1899. He found another job, with the Drouet Institute for the Deaf, and there he met an eighteen-year-old typist, Ethel le Neve.

On the night of 31 January 1910 the Crippens gave a party at Hilldrop Crescent. Shortly after the party had ended Dr Crippen poisoned his wife with a dose of hyoscin hydrobromide. He then cut up her body and buried it in the cellar beneath the house. Six weeks later, he took Ethel le Neve, who by then was his mistress, to live with him in Hilldrop Crescent. Friends and neighbours became suspicious about Belle's disappearance and their gossip brought a visit from the police. Crippen panicked and with Ethel tried to escape to Canada. She cut her hair short and dressed as a boy. They made their way to Antwerp where they boarded a boat, the Canadian Pacific liner *Montrose*, in the names of Mr and Master Robinson. The police found the dismembered body and a reward was offered for information which would help in the arrest of Crippen and le Neve. The captain of the *Montrose* read an account of the disappearance of Crippen and le Neve in a newspaper and immediately became suspicious of his two passengers, Mr and Master Robinson. He sent a wireless message to Scotland Yard—the first time wireless was used to catch a criminal. As a result, a Scotland Yard detective was able to take a faster ship, the *Laurentic*, and arrive in Canada before the *Montrose*. The detective boarded the *Montrose* and arrested Crippen and Ethel le Neve before they landed in Canada.

They were brought back to England, and at their trial which opened at the Old Bailey on 8 October 1910, Crippen was found guilty of murder and Ethel le Neve, not guilty. Crippen was hanged at Pentonville Prison, London, on 23 November 1910.

Dr Fell

I do not love thee, Dr Fell,
The reason why I cannot tell;
But this I know, and know full well,
I do not love thee, Dr Fell.

DR JOHN FELL (1625-86) was the dean of Christ Church College, Oxford. He was a strict disciplinarian and in 1670 he expelled Thomas Brown, an unruly student. He immediately relented and said that he would remit the sentence if Brown could give him an impromptu translation of Martial's 32nd epigram: *Non amo te, Sabidi, nec possum dicere quare; hoc tantum possum dicere, non amo te*—I do not like thee, Sabidius, but I cannot say why; I only know I do not like thee.

Thomas Brown straightway made his facetious translation, shown above. Fortunately Dr Fell had a sense of humour. He kept his word and remitted the sentence of expulsion. Six years after this incident, Dr Fell was made Bishop of Oxford without having to give up his deanery. He had been made dean of Christ Church and royal chaplain at the Restoration in reward for having served in the Royalist army and maintaining Anglican services at Oxford throughout Cromwell's commonwealth.

This same Dr Fell was interested in typography and is also remembered for his generosity in presenting the University Press with his huge collection of type which contained punches and matrices of various founts, including Arabic, Syriac, Coptic and the famous 'Fell' Roman.

Dr James Barry

THERE WAS NOTHING EXTRAORDINARY about Dr James Barry during his lifetime, except that he was a first-class surgeon and had a long and distinguished career as a medical officer in the British Army.

He was born in Scotland about 1792 and at the age of sixteen was enrolled as a medical student at the male-only Edinburgh University. He qualified in 1812 and immediately joined the Army as a medical officer. He was sent to South Africa and soon gained his reputation as a surgeon when, without antiseptics, he carried out the first successful caesarian operation there. As Colonial Medical Inspector he improved the sanitary conditions in prisons and leper colonies and imposed strict control on apothecaries and the supply of drugs. Once he was court-martialled for trying to improve the conditions of women hospital patients.

Dr Barry's career progressed and he served in the West Indies and India as well as South Africa. Eventually he was promoted to Inspector-General Surgeon to the British Army. He was a very popular, competent doctor and a very handsome one, too. The ladies liked him and in his youth he was wounded in a duel which he fought with a fellow officer over a woman.

When Dr Barry retired from the Army he lived in London, where he died on 25 July 1865. And it was then discovered that this eminent Army medical officer was a woman named Miranda Stuart. It was also revealed, at a post-mortem examination, that she had at some time very early in her life, given birth to a child. What happened to the child, or why Dr Barry chose to hide her true identity, is not known and remains one of those unsolved mysteries of life.

Dr Jekyll

SOME OF THE MOST bizarre characters in fiction are modelled on a reality, and the man upon whom Robert Louis Stevenson based his famous character of Dr Jekyll was William Brodie, a respected Scottish businessman.

Brodie, who was born in Edinburgh about 1741, was the son of a rich cabinet-maker. As a city councillor and deacon, or leader, of the mason's guild he was held in high esteem in the prudish city where he lived. But this model of virtue had a secret life which nobody knew about. So close was his secret that the two mistresses he kept did not even know about it. In fact they did not even know about each other— and yet between them they had borne Brodie five children. By day Deacon Brodie, as he was called, was a respected businessman and a doer of good works, but by night he was a gambler and a thief.

His life of crime began at the age of twenty-seven when he robbed a bank of £800. For eighteen years he continued to burgle without being found out. But, like most thieves, he was eventually to make a mistake. In 1786, he teemed up with three petty thieves and together they planned to raid the headquarters of the Scottish Customs and Excise. Their plan went wrong and they were surprised by a customs official. Brodie got away and fled to Amsterdam, intending to make his way to America. But unfortunately for him, one of the others, John Brown, turned King's evidence to save himself from being transported for other crimes he had committed in England.

Police caught up with Brodie in Amsterdam the night before he was to leave for America. He was extradited and sent for trial in Edinburgh. He stood in the dock in the same courtroom where, a short while earlier, he had sat as a juryman. Brodie's game was up and his double identity revealed. Police had found a burglar's black suit, false keys and guns. There was no chance for him, and he was sentenced to death and hanged on 1 October 1788.

In *The Strange Case of Dr Jekyll and Mr Hyde* Robert Louis Stevenson shows that evil can be in every man and that often it can override the goodness in him, as it did in the case of the good Deacon Brodie.

Dr Spooner

'Kinquering congs their titles take'

ONE OF THE MOST wrongly ridiculed characters in recent history is Dr Spooner. He is thought of simply as a metathetic who bumbled his way through life, tripping over his words and giving his name to the word 'spoonerism', which was included in the dictionary in his own lifetime. But while Dr Spooner did have a tendency to misplace some of his words (the above quote is the best-known example), he was certainly no bumbling idiot. In fact he was a doctor of divinity and the Warden of New College, Oxford.

William Archibald Spooner was born in London on 22 July 1844. At the age of eighteen he won an open scholarship from Oswestry School to New College, Oxford. He took two first-class degrees—in classical moderations and humanities— and spent the rest of his life at the college. He was elected fellow in 1867, lecturer in 1868, tutor in 1869, dean in 1876, having been ordained priest the previous year, and Warden in 1903, the year in which he took his Doctor of Divinity degree. He was also an examiner for various colleges, university boards and chaplaincies.

As a tutor and a priest he was greatly admired by his students and contemporaries. He lectured on ancient history, philosophy, especially on Aristotle's *Ethics*, and divinity. He was eloquent and his speeches and sermons were interesting and amusing. Some of his speech lapses probably resulted from the difficulty he sometimes had in reading since, being an albino, he suffered from defective eyesight. Many spoonerisms have been coined since Dr Spooner's day and it is hardly likely that he admonished a student, 'you are always hissing at my mystery lessons', or that he rode round Oxford on his 'well-boiled icicle'.

In 1878 Dr Spooner married Frances Wycliffe, daughter of the Bishop of Carlisle, and they had two sons and five daughters. For almost seventy years he was a loved and respected character in the City of Oxford and his highly esteemed opinion on university affairs carried great weight. He died on 29 August 1930, aged eighty-six, and is buried at Grasmere, Cumbria, where his wife's house, How Foot, had for many years been a favourite holiday home.

El Cid

El Cid, that mighty man of war
Feared no-one,
Least of all a Moor.

EL CID WAS THE title given to Rodriguez Dias de Bivar, a Spanish nobleman who fought for Christian Spain against the Moors in the eleventh century. The word 'Cid' is a corruption of the Arabic word 'seyyid', meaning lord.

Rodriguez was born near Burgos in northern Spain, in 1043. In 1065, when Sancho II became King of Castile, he appointed El Cid marshal of the royal army, which El Cid led to victory against Sancho's brother, Alfonso VI of Leon. El Cid remained the king's favourite until Sancho was murdered, probably by his brother who succeeded him as Alfonso I of Castile.

Rodriguez served under Alfonso for a short while until they quarrelled and Alfonso banished him. With a band of vassals El Cid headed for Valencia and defended eastern Spain against the Moors. When Al Qadir, King of Valencia, died in 1094, El Cid became ruler and remained so until his death in 1099 at the age of fifty-six.

El Cid, who was also known as El Campeador—the champion—married Alfonso's niece, Doña Jimena Diaz, in 1074 and by her had twin daughters, who married the princes of Navarre and Aragon.

Elizabeth Fry

IN NINETEENTH-CENTURY ENGLAND, women like Elizabeth Fry and Florence Nightingale (see p85) stood apart from all others. They were reformers whose love for the underprivileged caused them to abandon the life of luxury they had been born into. At first they were thought to be priggish and their chosen work fit only for the rabble, but their dedication and perseverance changed the opinions of society, and in their own lifetimes they were revered as angels of mercy.

Elizabeth Fry was born in Norwich on 21 May 1780 and was the daughter of John Gurney, a rich Quaker merchant banker. She grew up with all the advantages of the moneyed classes, but also with a sense of mission. By the time she was seventeen she was despairing of ever having anything worthwhile to do and in her diary she wrote: 'If some kind and great circumstance does not happen to me I shall have my talents devoured by moth and rust.'

The kind and great circumstance happened a year later, for she set up her own school to teach poor and uneducated children. She even visited their homes and was appalled by the conditions in which they lived—conditions far removed from her comfortable surroundings. In 1800, at the age of twenty, she married Joseph Fry, a member of another leading Quaker family. By 1816 she had had ten children. But she was not really cut out for the humdrum existence of domesticity and motherhood alone, and after the third child she wrote in her diary: 'It does appear to me that I might become the careworn and oppressed mother.' She tried to do good works whenever she could and began preaching with such persuasive effect that by 1811 she was appointed an 'approved minister' of the Society of Friends (Quakers).

In 1813 she was encouraged by Stephen Gellett, a French aristocratic Quaker, to go to Newgate Prison to see the appalling conditions in which the women prisoners were forced to live.

Her children grew more and more out of hand, and devoted mother though she was she described them as 'naughty and trying noisy brats'. It was almost a relief to her when, in 1816, her husband's business difficulties caused the family income to drop and she had to farm most of her children out to relations. Elizabeth could now concentrate her energies on what came most naturally to her—working for the oppressed. She went back to Newgate Prison with the intention of doing something for the women and their children. Despite the governor's warnings, she went inside to talk to the violent, desperate women. She arranged for a school to be set up in a room in the prison and for the women prisoners to run it under the supervision of a committee of eleven Quaker women whom she enlisted to help her improve prison conditions. She wanted to give the prisoners back their self-respect and prepare them for the day when they would be released. She refused to believe that prisoners were foul, animal-like creatures not worth helping, and within a year she had triumphed. Prison reform was on the way. In 1818 she won great acclaim by being the first woman to be invited to give evidence before the House of Commons Committee on Prisons. Much notice was taken of her reforms and she became an admired public figure. But life was not always easy for her. She had her opponents and when people wanted to hurt her they accused her of being a neglectful mother, always dashing off to help others.

Besides fighting for prison reform she did what she could to help convicts who were being transported to the colonies. Between 1818 and 1843 she visited 106 ships and ensured that 1,200 people set off in better conditions than they might otherwise have done. Her care was not limited just to England. She visited prisons in Scotland and Ireland, and in 1821 she wrote a report on prison reform which brought official inquiries from Russia, Italy and Denmark. She founded a shelter for the homeless in winter, fought for better treatment of the mentally ill and founded a training school for Fry Nurses, some of whom went to the Crimea with Florence Nightingale.

Her good work extended overseas. In 1829, as a result of her efforts, a law was passed to prohibit suttee (the burning of a widow on her husband's pyre) in India. Between 1838 and 1843 she was invited to France, Switzerland, Germany, Holland, Belgium and Denmark to visit the prisons and give her advice.

Between all these works of mercy she gave birth to an eleventh child in 1822. She died on 12 October 1845 at Ramsgate in Kent.

The Emperor Norton

His Imperial Majesty, Norton, I, Dei Gratia
Emperor of the United States and Protector of Mexico

WHEN THE AMERICANS FOUGHT their War of Independence, they little realised that, less than a century later, they would be 'ruled' by an Englishman again. The Emperor Norton I began his reign in September 1859, when he told the editor of the *San Francisco Bulletin*: 'I am the Emperor of the United States.' Amused by the seriousness of the down-and-out in the shabby army colonel's uniform, the editor decided to publish his proclamation on the front page. The San Franciscans were equally amused and so began the reign of His Imperial Majesty Norton I, that was to last for twenty years.

Joshua Abraham Norton was born in London in 1819, and two years later his family emigrated to South Africa where his father, a farmer and ship's chandler, helped to pioneer Grahamstown. Norton grew up to head a vast commercial empire, but when his father died in 1848, he sold his business and moved to Brazil. A year later he went to San Francisco as he had heard that gold had been discovered in California, but when he arrived he thought he would make money more quickly by opening a store in the booming city than by panning for gold. In four years he had made a quarter of a million dollars. But Norton was not satisfied. He decided to corner the market in rice and bought up every cargo. The price soared to 50 cents a lb, but he would not sell. Then unexpectedly cargo ships arrived from South America laden with rice and the market collapsed. Two years later Norton was bankrupt. And he was still bankrupt, and somewhat more eccentric, when he issued his first proclamation to the editor of the *Bulletin*.

Norton continued to make proclamations and the people of San Francisco were delighted. He declared that because of corruption the President was deposed and Congress abolished, and that in future he would rule in person. He ordered the US Army to proceed with suitable force and clear the Halls of Congress. He then issued a proclamation that because the Mexicans were incapable of managing their own affairs, he was henceforth 'Protector of Mexico' as well.

Each morning he held court in the lodging house where he lived. On his walls were pictures of Napoleon and Queen Victoria. In the afternoon he wandered the streets, accompanied by his two dogs, checking such things as drains and bus timetables, and acknowledging the deep bows of his respectful subjects. Each Sunday he went to a different church to avoid jealousy among the various denominations. He was given free travel, free meals and he had his own seat at the theatre. Never having any money he levied a tax of 25 to 30 cents a week for shopkeepers and $3 for banks, and most of them gamely paid up.

The San Franciscans were loyal subjects and when the Emperor issued a proclamation for new clothes: 'Know ye that we, Norton the First, have diverse complaints from our liege subjects that our Imperial wardrobe is a national disgrace', they voted funds for a new uniform.

Perhaps it is surprising that Norton was never arrested. But he was once, for vagrancy, by an over-eager young policeman. The whole city was furious, and Norton was released by the Chief of Police personally, with profuse apologies. The city then sent a deputation to apologise and Norton graciously agreed to 'blot the incident from my memory'.

Norton died on 8 January 1880 and 10,000 people filed past his coffin in two days. His obituary in the *Bulletin* read: 'The Emperor Norton killed nobody, robbed nobody and deprived nobody of his country—which is more than can be said for most fellows in his trade.' That obviously, was the secret of his attraction. In 1934, a headstone was placed on his grave in Woodlawn Cemetery, with the inscription: 'Norton I, Emperor of the United States, Protector of Mexico, 1819–1880.'

Fabius Maximus

WHEN WE TALK ABOUT Fabian tactics we mean a strategy based on the gradual wearing down of the enemy or opposition. And the man who gave his name to the expression was the Roman general and consul, Fabius Maximus Verrucosus.

Fabius was made dictator of Rome in 217 BC when Hannibal and his Carthaginian army were invading Italy during the second Punic War (see p66). Hannibal had severely beaten the Romans at the Battle of Trasimene and was fast advancing upon Rome. Fabius, who had only a small force at his command, did not dare to engage in pitched battles but resorted to delaying tactics until he could assemble enough men to defend the city successfully. He kept to the hills and hampered the enemy's progress by cutting off their food and supply lines with small surprise attacks. These delaying tactics earned him the name of 'Cunctator'—the Delayer.

Fabius managed to hold off Hannibal until the Romans had gathered their strength and morale and were able to triumphantly defend their city. At the time, Fabius's tactics were disapproved of by his soldiers and the civilians and to emphasise their disapproval they elected his master-of-the-horse co-dictator. But later his wisdom was appreciated and he continued to play an important part in the war.

Fabius died in 203 BC, but his name lives on.

During the American War of Independence, George Washington used similar tactics to those of Fabius and became known as the American Fabius. The word Fabian was also used by a group of middle-class intellectuals who founded a society (the Fabian Society) in January 1884 to advance the principles of socialism. Among the prominent members were George Bernard Shaw, Sidney Webb and Annie Besant, and they took the name Fabian as they believed that it would take a long time, advancing by small degrees and avoiding an open breach with capitalism, until they had enough power to reach their objective.

Fanny Burney

IN 1817, COMTE ALEXANDRE D'ARBLAY, a retired émigré officer, went to Paris to have his portrait painted by the brothers Carle and Horace Vernet. 'All the world will tell Alex who his mother is', he said, 'but so that he shall not forget who his father was I have had this portrait painted which I dedicate to him.' A year later d'Arblay died and but for his wife, the celebrated diarist, Fanny Burney, whom all the world would tell of, he might well have sunk into obscurity.

Fanny, who was born in King's Lynn, Norfolk, in 1752, was one of the nine children of Dr Charles Burney, the eminent musician and composer. Among Dr Burney's friends who often came to his house in London were Dr Johnson, Sir Joshua Reynolds, David Garrick and Edmund Burke, and Fanny grew up among these distinguished people. As a child she read English and French literature and began to write herself. She scribbled great screeds of poems, stories, plays and songs and when she was fifteen she made a bonfire of the lot. Among the stories destroyed was one which she later rewrote from memory and which formed the basis of her first published book, *Evelina*.

Evelina, Or the History of a Young Lady's Entrance Into the World was one of the first novels to deal with domestic and social life. Since it was not the done thing for women in those days to write books, it was published anonymously in 1778. It was an immediate success, and when Fanny heard her father's eminent friends praising it, she confessed to the authorship. Dr Johnson and other critics lionised her and she then began writing under her own name. She encouraged other women writers, particularly Jane Austen, but her own future novels never met with the success of *Evelina*.

In 1786, to please her devoutly royalist father, she accepted a post at court as second Keeper of the Robes to Queen Charlotte. She hated every minute of court life as she was bullied by fellow courtiers, particularly Madame Schwellenberg, her immediate superior. Nevertheless, she found time to carry on writing the diary she had begun in earlier years, which was to become her masterpiece and send her into fame. Her health was suffering at court and in 1791 she was allowed to retire on a small pension. Two years later she married Comte d'Arblay, a French army general. It was to prove a happy marriage.

Besides her novels and diary, Fanny wrote a biography of her father, but it is her lively diary, which contains sketches of Dr Johnson and David Garrick, for which she is best remembered.

The Flanders Mare

The King found her so different from her picture ... he swore they had brought him a Flanders mare.

THE UNFLATTERING TITLE OF the Flanders Mare belonged to a Queen of England, Anne of Cleves—and it was given to her by her husband-to-be, Henry VIII.

When Henry was casting his sights for yet another bride after the natural death of his adored third wife, Jane Seymour, he sent the court painter, Hans Holbein, to Holland to paint portraits of Anna and Amelia, the two unmarried daughters of the Duke of Cleves. Both were beautiful portraits, but Henry chose Anna, afterwards called Anne.

English politicians were delighted that Henry had chosen a bride from an ardent Protestant family. England, joined to the League of Protestant Princes, would be all the more powerful against the Catholic monarchs of Austria, Spain and France. But a union was to be short-lived.

Anne was well educated, although she could not sing or speak any language other than her native Dutch. Henry had been led to believe that she was talented and beautiful, and he could not wait to meet her. When she arrived at Rochester in Kent on New Year's Eve, 1539,

Henry disguised himself as a messenger and took her a New Year's gift 'from the King'. Anne was not impressed by the overweight nobleman who was paying his respects and Henry was affronted. Henry too was not impressed with what he saw. Anne was not what he had been led to believe she was. No one had told him that she was large and ungainly, big boned and pock marked. 'I am ashamed that men have so praised her as they have done—and I like her not. She is a great Flanders mare,' Henry told Thomas Cromwell, his chief adviser.

Henry knew that he could never love Anne, and although he tried unsuccessfully to find a legal means of getting out of the marriage, the wedding took place on 6 January 1540. 'The most miserable Twelfth Night of my life', he afterwards said. But neither was it a happy day for Anne. She was timid and scared of the great colossus she had married. She and Henry were married in name only for their marriage was never consummated. Anne's only happiness was found with the royal children—Mary, Elizabeth and little Edward—to whom she endeared herself.

Soon Henry was tiring of his unexciting Flanders mare and was beginning to show interest in one of Anne's ladies-in-waiting, Catherine Howard. He decided to divorce Anne after about five months of marriage. Anne was only too willing to agree to a divorce. Shortly afterwards Henry married Catherine Howard, who survived as queen for just eighteen months, and was then beheaded when Henry became aware of the misdeeds of her past life.

After the divorce Anne continued to live at Richmond and remained on friendly terms with all the royal family, including Henry's next two wives. Her relationship with Henry was that of brother and sister. When she died in 1557, Mary, who was queen at the time, ordered that she should have a royal funeral and be buried in Westminster Abbey—the only one of Henry's six queens to lie there.

Hans Holbein's portrait, which decided the marriage, can be seen in the Victoria & Albert Museum in London.

The Führer

THE FÜHRER WAS ADOLF HITLER, the Austrian-born demagogue and leader of Germany's Third Reich who, although claiming to be a man of peace, plunged Europe into World War II and committed suicide as the conflict came to an end.

He was born on 20 April 1889 at Braunau in Austria and was the son of a minor customs official who had changed his surname from Schicklgruber to Hitler. In 1907 he went to Vienna where he hoped to become an architect or a painter, but he failed to get into art school and worked as an artisan. He was living in poverty and it was then that his anti-semitic and anti-marxist views evolved. In 1912 he went to Munich, and at the outbreak of World War I he joined the German Army and rose to the rank of corporal. He was awarded the Iron Cross for services as a runner on the western front, and at the time of the armistice in 1918 he was lying in hospital, temporarily blinded, having been wounded and gassed.

In 1919, full of bitterness at Germany's defeat, he became the seventh member of an extremist group known as the German Worker's Party. By 1921 he had become leader of the party. He changed its name to the National Socialist German Worker's Party, which was abbreviated to Nazi, and instituted a new political programme based on challenging established law and order and aiming to overthrow the Bavarian government. But his *putsch*, or revolt, was an utter failure and Hitler was sentenced to five years imprisonment. He was released after nine months, but during that time he wrote the major part of his famous book *Mein Kampf* (My Struggle), which was his vision for the future of Germany.

In 1929 when the German economy collapsed, Hitler won mass support from the German people. He promised work to the unemployed and by 1930 his Nazi party had become the second largest party in the Reichstag. Two years later it was the largest, and in 1933 President Hindenburg appointed Hitler Chancellor of Germany. He outlawed or suppressed all other political parties and quickly turned Germany into a one-party state. He was voted complete dictatorial power and in 1934, after Hindenburg's death, he assumed the title of Führer (leader). He launched a massive rearmament programme and determined to avenge Germany for the shame suffered by its defeat in World War I, and to re-establish the supremacy of the Aryan race. By 1936 he was ready to 'conquer Europe' and so expand German territory. He sent troops into the Rhineland in 1936, Austria in 1938 and Czechoslovakia in 1939. Finally, he invaded Poland and precipitated World War II.

His early military triumphs, when he was virtually master of the European continent, were reversed by heavy defeats in Russia and North Africa in 1942-3. He survived an attempt by anti-Nazis to assassinate him on 20 July 1944, but when Berlin fell to the Russians in 1945, he committed suicide in a bunker on 30 April, ten days after his fifty-sixth birthday.

Although Hitler was an absolute dictator, he was neither a great statesman nor a military genius. But he was one of the greatest demagogues in history and his rasping harangues had the power to infuse into millions of Germans a wild fanaticism equal to his own. He was cunning and clever, but much of his power depended upon the efficient administration of his subordinates such as Goebbels, Goering, Himmler and Ribbentrop.

Garibaldi

GIUSEPPE GARIBALDI WAS AN Italian patriot who was partly responsible for the unification and independence of Italy. He was born in Nice on 4 July 1807, and was the son of a poor fisherman. As a young man he joined Mazzini's Young Italy movement—a group intent on uniting Italy—and because of his involvement in an attempt to seize Genoa in 1834 was forced to flee to South America. There he volunteered to fight for the Province of Rio Grande against the Emperor of Brazil. He was becoming well known as a revolutionary soldier and in 1843 he commanded the forces defending Montevideo against the army of the United Provinces from Buenos Aires.

Despite his revolutionary activities he found time to marry the creole Anita Riviera de Silva, the companion of his earlier campaigns and the mother of his three children. In 1848 he returned to Italy and the following year commanded the troops defending the Roman Republic against the French. The Republic was defeated and in 1850 Garibaldi escaped to the United States, where he became a naturalised citizen and worked as a candlemaker in New York City. In 1854 he returned to Italy and settled down as a farmer at Caprera until 1859, when he swore allegiance to King Victor Emmanuel and led the guerillas against the Austrians in northern Italy. In 1860 he sailed from Genoa with his famous band of 1,000 men, known as the Red Shirts, and successfully invaded Sicily and Naples, driving out the Bourbons. His dream was coming true—he had formed the nucleus of a United Italy, and Victor Emmanuel was proclaimed king. He then marched north, but failed in his two attempts to conquer Rome and the Papal states, in 1862 and 1867. Later he led a volunteer force in the Franco-Prussian War. He then retired to his farm at Caprera where he spent much of his time writing manifestoes.

Garibaldi died on 2 June 1882, and was mourned throughout Italy and Europe as a man who had given his life to the cause of liberty.

Gordon Bennett

THE EXPRESSION 'GORDON BENNETT!' is often used as an exclamation of amazement or even as a mild expletive, so it may come as a surprise to know that there really was a Gordon Bennett. In fact, there were two—father and son. But it was the wild, eccentric younger Bennett who caused his name to live on eponymously.

James Gordon Bennett was born in New York City on 10 May 1841. His father was a Scottish immigrant who eventually settled in New York and became the proprietor of the New York *Herald*. Bennett was educated in Paris, but returned to America when the Civil War began and joined the Union navy. Later he joined his father's business, and when the elder Bennett died in 1872, Gordon inherited the newspaper. He was a confident, brilliant journalist, but erratic and unpredictable. He kept tight control over his newspaper, making all major decisions himself, even though he spent most of his time in Paris after 1877. He changed the paper into a reflection of his own tastes, devoting much coverage to international affairs, sport and social events. He added excitement to the paper by financing various expeditions, the most notable of which was sending Stanley to Africa to search for Dr Livingstone. He was a keen sportsman and introduced polo to America. He competed in the first transatlantic yacht race in 1866, and donated cups for balloon, motor car and aeroplane competitions. He also had an active social conscience, and during the financial troubles of 1873 he opened free kitchens in New York's poorer districts. In 1882 he donated $100,000 to start the *Herald* Relief Fund for Irish Sufferers.

For almost a quarter of a century he was enterprising enough to maintain the *Herald* as a quality paper, but eventually his egotism, extravagant behaviour and lavish spending undermined its image. Bennett's behaviour was always a source of consternation to his companions, and eventually he quarrelled with his staff and with other newspaper proprietors to such an extent that while other newspapers were expanding, the *Herald*'s circulation was waning. As the life of the old man was ebbing away, so was the circulation of the *Herald*. Bennett died at Beaulieu, France, on 14 May 1918.

One of the rawest tales told about Gordon Bennett happened on New Year's Day, 1877. Already drunk, he arrived at a party being given at the Fifth Avenue home of his fiancée, Caroline May. After more drinking, he unbuttoned his fly in front of all the guests and urinated into the blazing fire. Bennett was taken by the scruff of the neck and thrown into the street. Next day Caroline's brother Frederick horsewhipped Bennett outside his club, and this led to a duel which fortunately ended without bloodshed. From then on, most of the respectable homes were closed to Bennett and he took refuge in France. And here he gave rise to yet another famous story. He arrived at a restaurant without a reservation and was very annoyed to find that all the tables were occupied. Rather than wait, he sought out the owner and bought the restaurant on the spot for a million francs, which he paid in cash. He then ordered a table to be cleared immediately, and sat down to his favourite meal of mutton chops. After the meal he gave the deeds of the restaurant to the waiter, telling him that there must always be a table ready for Gordon Bennett and that there must always be mutton chops on the menu.

No wonder people shook their heads and in desperation said: 'Gordon Bennett!'

Grace Darling

GRACE DARLING WAS AN English heroine, who defied perilous seas to rescue survivors from a wrecked steamboat.

Grace, who was born at Bamburgh in Northumberland on 24 November 1815, was the daughter of William Darling, the keeper of the Longstone Lighthouse on the Farne Islands. With her eight brothers and sisters she was brought up very strictly, as her father was a man of strong puritan principles.

On 7 September 1838 the steamboat *Forfarshire* was wrecked upon a rock in raging seas and forty-three people were drowned. From his lighthouse, William Darling saw that some survivors had taken refuge on a rock. Disregarding the tempest that was raging, Grace implored her father to go to the rescue. So he launched their small boat and they both rowed out to the rock. They brought back four men and a woman to the lighthouse. Then, with the help of two of the rescued men, William rowed out again and brought back the four remaining men.

Reports of their gallant rescue brought rewards and praise from all sources. The Humane Society presented them with gold medals and the Treasury awarded Grace £50 for her bravery. The general public showed their appreciation and admiration by sending in over £1,000 and £750 was invested for Grace and £270 for her father—quite a lot of money for those days. People even wrote and asked for locks of Grace's hair and the proprietor of a circus tried to engage her.

Fortunately Grace remained unaffected by her popularity which was just as well for, a shorter than average girl, she had never been very strong in health. She suddenly developed tuberculosis and died on 20 October 1842, one month before her twenty-seventh birthday. She is buried at Bamburgh, where there is also a museum devoted to her.

Guy Fawkes

Guy, Guy, stick him up on high,
Tie him to a lamppost
And there let him die.

AS NOVEMBER APPROACHES, London children can be heard chanting this, or another, ditty as they parade an effigy of Guy Fawkes, pausing only to ask the passers-by, 'Penny for the Guy, please?'

But who on earth *was* Guy Fawkes? Ask any of these children, and few will know the answer. He was not a Spaniard, as is commonly supposed. He was in fact a Yorkshireman—the only son of an Anglican lawyer who was employed by the Anglican Church Courts in the city of York. Guy was baptised in the Anglican church of St Michael-le-Belfry, York on 10 April 1570. When he was nine, his father died and shortly afterwards his mother married a Roman Catholic named Dionis Baynbrigge. Guy became greatly influenced by his Catholic surroundings, particularly at St Peter's School which he now attended. He converted to Catholicism and when he became of age in 1591, he sold his property in York and two years later went off to Flanders to join the Spanish Army. He proved himself a very able soldier and won distinction at the siege of Calais in 1595.

By now his devotion to Catholicism was almost fanatical, and his one aim in life was to restore papal supremacy in England. In 1603, when Queen Elizabeth I was dying, Sir William Stanley, commander of the English Catholic troops in the Spanish Army in the Netherlands, sent Guy Fawkes to Spain to try to persuade Philip III to secure relief for his fellow Catholic countrymen.

Fawkes then returned to England, and when James I acceded to the throne the gunpowder plot was hatched. James had declared himself in favour of persecution of the Catholics and Guy and his fellow conspirators, William Catesby, Thomas Percy and Thomas Winter among them, vowed to blow up the King and the Houses of Parliament. Fawkes, who was really nothing more than a manipulated puppet in the plot, agreed to light the gunpowder, vowing to do the dirty deed even if he perished in the act. But the plot was discovered and Guy Fawkes was arrested as he entered the gunpowder-filled cellar beneath the Houses of Parliament on the night of 4–5 November 1605. At first he refused to reveal the names of his fellow conspirators, but his resolution broke under severe torture and he gave their names, although some of them had already been arrested. The conspirators were tried and found guilty, and Guy Fawkes, together with some of the others, was hanged from a scaffold opposite the Houses of Parliament on 31 January 1606.

Since Guy intended to blow up the King as well as Parliament, the sovereign's 'seat' is still ceremoniously searched at the State Opening of Parliament.

Hannibal

'I, Hannibal, swear that so soon as age will permit, I will follow the Romans both at sea and on land. I will use fire and steel to arrest the destiny of Rome!'

HANNIBAL WAS A CARTHAGINIAN general who spent his whole life fighting Rome. His father, Hamilcar Barca, also a Carthaginian general, had crossed into Spain in 241 BC in the hope of building up an empire after he had lost the first Punic War against Italy. Hannibal was nine years old, and his father took him to the temple at Peñíscola, to the north of Valencia, where Hannibal laid his hand upon the altar and swore his solemn oath of enmity. Thirteen years later, Hamilcar died, and his son-in-law, Hasdrubal, took command.

Hannibal, now in his twenties, took part in a lot of fighting and proved himself a courageous soldier and clever tactician. Then Hasdrubal was assassinated, and Hannibal assumed command. He precipitated the second Punic War by attacking Saguntum, a Spanish ally of Rome. He besieged the city for eight months, and when they saw that defeat was inevitable the people of Saguntum, rather than surrender to the Carthaginians, set fire to their city and committed mass suicide.

Hannibal, who never forgot the oath he had sworn as a child, was now ready for his most cherished ambition—to fight Rome on her own soil. He gathered together a huge army consisting of 90,000 infantrymen, 12,000 cavalrymen and 37 elephants, together with mules to carry the baggage. In May 218 BC his great army moved northwards from Cartagena, through Spain, across France and over the Alps via the Little St Bernard Pass into Italy. Although Hannibal lost many men and animals on the journey, he and the elephants arrived safely. In 217 BC he defeated the Romans at Trasimene, and in 216 at Cannae. He continued to fight in Italy, but was being worn down by Fabius Maximus's cunctatory (delaying) tactics (see p54) which avoided open battle, and in 203 BC he returned to Africa to defend Carthage against the invasion by Scipio Africanus. He was finally defeated by Scipio at Zama in 202. Carthage made a disastrous peace and Hannibal remained in power until Rome demanded his life in 195, and he went into exile in Asia. In 182 BC, he committed suicide to avoid capture.

In September 1979, a group of Americans, led by a Los Angeles philosophy professor and his fiancée, retraced Hannibal's footsteps over the Alps, in the company of two circus elephants.

Houdini

HARRY HOUDINI WAS AN American escapologist who could set himself free from any kind of prison or bodily hindrance. Among the things he escaped from during his career as an entertainer were handcuffs, fetters and chains, locked chambers, and sealed packing cases lowered into rivers, often beneath ice.

He was born in Wisconsin on 6 April 1874 and was the son of a Hungarian rabbi. His real name was Erich Weiss and he took his stage name from a French conjuror called Robert Houdin, whose biography he had read when he was a child.

Houdini was very interested in psychic phenomena and maintained that most of his acts, although they appeared to some people to be acts of reckless stupidity, were feats of precisely calculated skill combined with 'magic'.

He died in the USA on 31 October 1926 at the age of fifty-two, as the result of an act that went wrong. He was preparing his stomach muscles for a punch, when his eager accomplice punched too soon, Houdini was fatally injured and died from peritonitis as a result.

Inigo Jones

INIGO JONES WAS THE first English classical architect and a designer for masques at the courts of James I and Charles I.

The son of a clothworker, he was born in London in 1573. At the age of fourteen he was apprenticed for seven years to a joiner. Not much is known about his youth, except that he spent some years in Italy, mainly in Venice and Florence. He then went to Denmark at the command of King Christian IV, the first of his royal masters, where he was painter and designer to the royal court.

It was in this capacity that he joined the English court of James I and Queen Anne, King Christian's sister, when he returned to England about 1605. He turned his talents to architecture about 1608, and it is as an architect that he is best known.

He continued in the royal service, becoming Surveyor of the King's Works in 1615, and kept the appointment under the patronage of Charles I.

The elaborateness and ingenuity of Jones's theatrical designs greatly influenced later theatre designers. He introduced the proscenium arch and was the first person to use movable scenery on stage. His architectural works, which were noted for their elegance and beauty of proportion, were based on the works of the Italian Renaissance architect, Andrea Palladio, and this earned Jones the title of the 'English Palladio'. Jones himself described his buildings as 'solid, proportionable, masculine and unaffected'.

Among the buildings designed by Inigo Jones are the Queen's House at Greenwich which is now part of the National Maritime Museum, the Banqueting House at Whitehall and the Queen's chapel at St James's. He also designed the first English piazza, at Covent Garden, but this has been mainly replaced by Georgian and Victorian buildings.

Inigo Jones died on 21 June 1652 aged seventy-nine, 'through grief, as is well known', said John Webb, his deputy, 'for the fatal calamity of his dread master'. Charles I, whom Jones had loyally supported during the Civil War, had been executed three and a half years previously. Jones was buried with his parents in St Benet's Church, Paul's Wharf, London.

The Iron Duke

For this is England's greatest son,
He that gain'd a hundred fights,
Nor ever lost an English gun....

THE 'GREATEST SON' TO whom the poet Tennyson was referring was the Duke of Wellington, and great he was when it came to fighting for his country. But he was not always loved by everybody. He was given his nickname, the Iron Duke, after he had put iron shutters at the windows of his London house to protect them from stones being thrown by rebellious mobs, protesting against his opposition to parliamentary reform.

The Duke, whose name was Arthur Wellesley, was born in Dublin on 1 May 1769 and was the sixth child of the Earl and Countess of Mornington. His mother did not like him very much and called him 'that ugly boy Arthur'. His father, who had been a Professor of Music at Trinity College, Dublin, died when Arthur was twelve, and he became increasingly shy and lonely without him. He was sent to Eton, but was a poor scholar and his mother thought the fees a waste of money, so she sent him to a private tutor in Brussels and then to a military academy at Angers in France. She had decided that her ugly, clumsy boy was only 'fit food for powder', and must go into the Army. Poor Arthur had never even thought of becoming a soldier. He was an accomplished violinist and wanted to follow a musical career like his father. But he did as his mother wished, and in 1787 he joined a Highland regiment as an ensign. And so began his glorious career in which he was to become, in the words of Queen Victoria, 'the greatest man this country ever produced'.

He established his military reputation in India where he directed the wars against the Mahrattas, bringing peace to India and establishing British rule by December 1804. Then followed his arduous struggle against Napoleon, in the Peninsular War in particular, and culminating in his defeat of Napoleon at the Battle of Waterloo in 1815.

After Waterloo he became Commander-in-Chief of the allied army of occupation in France. By now he had been made a viscount, field marshal and a duke. He was a very rich man with property in several different countries, and he was the hero of England. But he was not popular in France, of course. In 1816 arsonists tried to burn him alive in his house and two years later he escaped an attempt by a would-be assassin. He returned to England in 1818 and became a politician. Ten years later, when Lord Goderich resigned as Prime Minister, King George IV asked him to form a government. He was reluctant but, ever dutiful, he did as he was asked, and became Prime Minister on 8 January 1828. In 1829 he passed the Catholic Relief Bill, which meant that Catholics could vote and also become MPs. This did not please the protestant Lord Winchilsea, who accused him of double-dealing and challenged him to a duel, which they fought in Battersea Park and fortunately survived each other's pistols. But the Duke was against parliamentary reform. He believed in the ruling classes and that to give the vote to the majority would lead to anarchy and mob rule. When he let his views be known by the words 'as long as I hold any station in the government of the country, I shall always feel it my duty to resist such measures', his popularity waned overnight and mobs began to stone his house.

When he resigned as Prime Minister in 1830 he spent the next two years in opposition fighting the Reform Bill. Finally, conceding defeat, he advised his followers in the House of Lords to support the bill, which was passed on 8 June 1832. Eventually he regained his hero's status. He was made Chancellor of Oxford University and Warden of the Cinque Ports. When he retired from active politics in 1846 he spent most of his time at Walmer Castle near Deal, the official residence of the Warden of the Cinque Ports, where he died, while sitting in an armchair, on 14 September 1852.

As a soldier the Duke was unequalled. He was the embodiment of common sense, but he was a very private person with tightly controlled emotions. He had few men friends and his marriage to Kitty Pakenham was not a happy one. He was a great disciplinarian and his wife and sons were frightened of him. So it is not surprising that many anecdotes have grown up around him, for anecdotes whether legendary or otherwise, are what help to keep a personality alive. But two of the most famous are known to be apocryphal—for the Duke did not say 'Up, Guards, and at 'em!' Neither did he claim that the Battle of Waterloo was won on the playing fields of Eton.

Ivan the Terrible

IVAN THE TERRIBLE WAS Ivan IV, Tsar of Russia from 1533 to 1584. He earned his notorious title because of his ferocious cruelty towards his enemies when satisfying his insatiable appetite for power and territory.

He became Grand Prince of Muscovy at the age of three, after the death of his father, Vasily III. When he was fourteen, in 1547, he had himself crowned and assumed the title of Tsar—a name derived from the Latin *Caesar*, an absolute monarch. In the same year he married Anastasia Romanov, whose family founded the Romanov dynasty sixty years later.

During the whole of his reign he engaged in a power struggle with the *boyars* (nobility) whom he distrusted since they treated him badly while he was a child ruler. Energetic, ruthless and power-mad, by 1555 he had consolidated the Muscovite state by crushing the Khanates of Kazan and Astrakhan and bringing the whole Volga valley within his power. He strengthened the central government by setting up a state within the Muscovite state. This new state, called the Oprichnina, had its own administration, courts and army, and was run by a ruthless security police force which Ivan created.

In 1560 Anastasia died and Ivan became increasingly unbalanced—a side of his nature which had been evident since youth. In 1564, one of his trusted counsellors, Prince Kurbsky, deserted him for the King of Poland, and this was too much for the neurotic ruler. He now felt treason was rife and set about eradicating it by imprisonment, torture and executions. But he alternated these fits of sadistic cruelty with bouts of religious fervour. During one of his fits of passion, in 1582, he killed his heir, also named Ivan. Ivan the Terrible died two years later and was succeeded by his heir's brother, Feodor.

Jemima Nicholas

KNOWN LOCALLY AS THE 'General of the Red Army', Jemima Nicholas saved Britain from a peasants' revolt in the late eighteenth century.

On 22 February 1797, a French expeditionary force of 1,400 troops led by an Irish-American adventurer named General Tate, landed at Strumble Head, near Fishguard in Wales. Tate was hoping to incite the peasants to rebel against the landowners and to dethrone King George III. But his troops were mostly ex-convicts and they stole drink from the inns and drunkenly set about ravaging farms and shops. Th local people were not strong enough in numbers to stop them and the invaders set up a headquarters in a farm near Goodwick. Two days later, Lord Cawdor mustered the Castlemartin Yeomanry and advanced on the invaders' refuge. But not before Jemima Nicholas, a local cobbler, gathered some local women together and charged the drunken invaders with pitchforks. The women were dressed in red cloaks and the French soldiers, thinking they were the British army, fled in terror.

Jemima Nicholas managed to round up twelve prisoners. The rest retreated to the beach below Goodwick, hoping to make their escape. But Lord Cawdor and his men were waiting for them, and the French surrendered. That was the last foreign invasion of Great Britain.

Jemima, who earned her nickname from the incident, died in 1832 and is buried at the Church of St Mary, Fishguard. An inscribed stone marks the spot on Goodwick beach where the invaders surrendered to Lord Cawdor.

Joan of Arc

JOAN OF ARC, the Maid of Orléans, was a French national heroine, who led the French army against the invading English in the fifteenth century and enabled the Dauphin, the rightful heir to the French throne, to become King as Charles VII.

Joan, a peasant girl, was born at Domrémy in north-east France, on the Feast of the Epiphany, 6 January 1412. She was not educated, but was intelligent and highly religious, having been taught the elements of religion by her mother. At the age of thirteen she began to hear voices, which she identified as those of St Michael, St Margaret and St Catherine.

The Hundred Years War was being waged and England had the upper hand; Henry VI of England had become King of France in 1422. When the English began their siege of Orléans in 1428, Joan's voices urged her to take up her stand against the enemy. Joan was convinced that she had been chosen to deliver France from the English and conduct the Dauphin to Reims Cathedral to be crowned the rightful King of France.

In 1429, having convinced the Dauphin of her sincerity, she dressed as a man in a suit of armour, and led the French army to victory at Orléans, driving out the English. She then led the King to Reims and stood beside him, her standard in her hand, while he was crowned King Charles VII of France, in July 1429.

Joan continued her military campaign, but the weak Charles did not support her with enough troops and her attempt to attack Paris early in 1430 failed. But undeterred, she headed for Compiègne which had been besieged by the Burgundians who were allies of the English. With her usual courage she threw herself into the defence of the city, but while leading a sortie from the gates in May 1430, she was cut off from the main body of her troops and captured by the Burgundians. She was imprisoned, and Charles, whom she had brought to the throne, made no attempt to save her. Six months later John of Luxembourg sold her to the English for 10,000 gold crowns.

Early in 1431 she was brought to trial at Rouen. The ecclesiastical court, presided over by the Bishop of Beauvais, charged her with sorcery and heresy. She was accused of wantonly cutting her hair, wearing men's clothing and blasphemous pride in regarding herself responsible directly to God rather than the Church.

Her interrogation lasted from 21 February to 17 March, and through it all Joan stood steadfast and resolute, arguing her defence. She was found guilty and sentenced to be burned at the stake. On 24 May, exhausted by the interrogation and suddenly frightened of the stake, she signed a recantation of her alleged sins and her sentence was commuted to life imprisonment. Six days later, on 30 May 1431, she repudiated her recantation and was taken to the market place at Rouen and publicly burned. Faithful to the end, she died uttering the name of Jesus three times.

In 1456, after confused legal proceedings to remove any doubt as to Charles's right to the throne, the judgement of the trial was reversed and Joan was officially declared innocent. In 1869 a movement was begun for her canonisation. She was beatified in 1909 and canonised by Pope Benedict XV on 9 May 1920—almost 500 years after her death.

John Peel

D'ye ken John Peel with his coat so grey
D'ye ken John Peel at the break o' day
D'ye ken John Peel when he's far, far away
With his hounds and his horn in the morning.

JOHN PEEL WAS A farmer and horse dealer who loved to hunt. There was nothing spectacular about him, except that he would ride to hounds at every opportunity, and had it not been for a friend, J. W. Graves, writing a song about him, he might well have slipped into history literally unsung. As it is, he is the most famous huntsman of all time.

He was born at Caldbeck in Cumberland on 24 September 1776. When he was twenty he eloped to Gretna Green and married his young sweetheart, Mary White. They set up home at Upton, near Caldbeck, and there they raised thirteen children.

John Peel first went hunting in 1803, when he was almost twenty-six. On his first hunt he had fifteen hounds, and three or four of them were his own. His favourite meets were Skiddaw and Messenger Mire, and his favourite time for hunting was early in the morning, 'when the sound of his horn brought me from my bed', wrote his friend, Graves.

Foxhunting in the Fells is usually on foot. In fact, according to one member of the hunting aristocracy, a horse would be as much out of place at a meet of a fell-side pack as a hippopotamus and be about as useful. But obviously John Peel did not always agree. He could often be seen riding a small pony with his knees almost up to the saddle. And he rode his horse into posterity. He died on 13 November 1854 aged seventy-eight, but not before the song was written about him and he had sung it himself—indeed, he was the first person ever to sing it. He is buried in Caldbeck churchyard and his ornate tombstone reveals that his wife Mary, three of their sons and one daughter are buried with him.

John Wilkes Booth

JOHN WILKES BOOTH WAS an American actor and the man who assassinated President Abraham Lincoln.

A strikingly handsome melancholy man, he was born in Bel Air, Maryland, on 10 May 1838. By the time he was seventeen he had joined his father and his brothers in the acting profession. He was mainly a Shakespearean actor and often appeared with his brothers, Edwin and Junius. But unlike his brothers, Booth was a Confederate sympathiser—championing the cause of the eleven states which withdrew from the Union during the American Civil War (1861-5). Being in favour of slavery, Booth developed an intense dislike of the anti-slavery President Lincoln and in 1865, with a bunch of fellow conspirators, he planned to kidnap him and hold him to ransom for the release of Confederate prisoners. But the plan failed because the President did not appear at the spot where the kidnap was to take place. The conspirators then decided to assassinate Lincoln and the whole of his cabinet. Booth was the one who was assigned to kill the President.

On 14 April 1865, Abraham Lincoln was sitting in a box at Ford's Theatre in Washington, DC, watching a performance of *Our American Cousin*. Booth knew the theatre well, for he had often acted on its stage. He entered the President's box and shot Lincoln through the head. Booth then leaped from the box on to the stage, breaking a small bone in his foot as he did so. He brandished a blood-stained knife, which he had used to wound one of the President's guards, crying, 'The South is Avenged', then made his escape.

Booth was free for almost a fortnight and during this time he kept a diary in which he explained his motives for killing the President: 'I struck for my country alone,' he wrote. He was caught in Bowling Green, Virginia, on 26 April 1865, after a barn in which he was hiding was set on fire. He was found shot through the head, but who shot him, or whether he shot himself, is not known.

Kemal Atatürk

ATATÜRK, MEANING FATHER TURK, was the name adopted by Mustafa Kemal, the first President of the Republic of Turkey who liberated his country from the rule of despotic sultans and transformed it into a westernised state.

Born in 1881 at Salonika in Greece, Atatürk was the son of a tax official. He was left in his mother's care when his father died, and at the age of twelve he ran away from school to join the military academy. He was an intelligent but reserved pupil, and a report on him said 'a boy with whom it is impossible to be intimate'. In 1899 he passed out with the rank of captain and became associated with the Young Turk movement. The Young Turks, who opposed the despotism of the sultans, were mostly young army officers like himself, but Atatürk could not get on with people and became involved in quarrels with the movement's leaders. In 1911 he went off alone to fight in Tripoli during the war with Italy. Later he fought in the Balkan wars of 1912-13. In World War I, although he disapproved of Turkey's hasty intervention (on the side of Germany), he was given command of the Turkish forces at Anafarta and was chiefly responsible for the British failure in the Dardanelles. Soon afterwards he was promoted to general.

After the war he refused to accept the humiliating peace terms. He headed a nationalist movement in Ankara in opposition to the Sultan's government in Istanbul. He drove the invading Greeks out of Turkey and ensured the independence of the new Turkish republic. When the sultan was deposed, Atatürk became the first president of the republic and remained president until his death in 1938.

He immediately set about effecting social changes. He disestablished the country from Islam and it became a secular state in which all religions were tolerated provided they did not interfere with politics. He abolished polygamy, banned oriental dress in favour of western clothes, emancipated women, introduced the Gregorian calendar and the Roman alphabet. In 1934 he made the adoption of surnames compulsory, and himself assumed the name Atatürk. Before this title, he had already had four other names: his personal name was Mustafa; then a schoolmaster added the name Kemal, meaning perfection. Pasha was added during the war of independence. Later he was given the title of Ghazi (the victorious).

A fearless, passionate man, he ruled as a dictator, believing his policies to be in the best interests of his country and his people.

King Canute

KING CANUTE WAS THE son of the Danish king, Sweyn Forkbeard. In 1013, when he was about eighteen or nineteen, he accompanied his father on a Viking raid to England against Ethelred the Unready. Ethelred was a weak king and Eadric Streona, a treacherous favourite, had hoodwinked the people into believing that it would be better to surrender to Sweyn than to live under the incompetent Ethelred. The people deserted Ethelred and he fled overseas. Sweyn then became king, but he died soon afterwards and the Vikings proclaimed Canute his successor as king of England.

The English soon realised their mistake and, expelling Canute, called Ethelred back to rule. In 1016 Ethelred died and his son, Edmund Ironside, became king. Canute, who had returned with his Viking army the previous year, fought many battles with him and although he lost most of them, he devastated Edmund at Ashingdon in Essex on 18 October 1016. The country was then divided between the two rivals, Canute taking the area north of the Thames. After Edmund's death six weeks later, on 30 November, Canute became king of all England.

Canute was a good, strong king. The transformation that took place after his accession was amazing. It is hard to believe that the civilised Christian ruler he became was the same person as the wild heathen pirate who had invaded England a few years previously. He married Ethelred's widow, Emma, was baptised as a Christian and became a devout member of the church. He sent his Danish army back to Denmark, keeping just a small bodyguard for himself, and employed Englishmen at court and in offices of state. He promoted some of the leaders of the English Church to bishops, patronised the abbeys of Winchester and Bury St Edmunds and made Godwin Earl of Wessex. He divided the country into earldoms, revised the laws and appointed sheriffs to keep them. He was accepted by the Scots and Welsh as their overlord, and honoured in Rome by Benedict VIII, Pope and Emperor. In 1019 he became king of Denmark and in 1028 king of Norway also.

The country improved under his wise rule and his subjects revered him. They thought him capable of anything. There is a legend that in an attempt to prove his humility to flattering subjects, some of whom suggested that he could even command the waves, he stood on the seashore and ordered back the tide. When the tide disobeyed and soaked his feet he said: 'Let all men know how empty and worthless is the power of kings, for there is none worthy of the name, but He whom heaven, earth and sea obey by eternal laws.' He is then said to have hung up his crown in Winchester Cathedral, never to wear it again.

Canute died on 12 November 1035 at Shaftesbury and is buried at Winchester. After this death, his kingdom broke up. Hardicanute, his son by Emma, became king of Denmark. He had two other sons, Sweyn and Harold, by his first wife, Aelgifu. Harold became king of England and Sweyn succeeded to Norway.

King Solomon

But when old age crept over them,
With many, many qualms,
King Solomon wrote the Proverbs
And King David wrote the psalms.

A WISE MAN IS often referred to as a Solomon, for King Solomon was considered to be the personification of wisdom. When he became king, at the behest of his dying father, King David, the Lord appeared to him in a dream bidding him to choose whatever gift he liked. Solomon chose an understanding heart so that he could judge the people's disputes and discern between good and evil. The Lord granted his wish, giving him a heart 'full of wisdom and discernment beyond all that went before thee or shall come after thee'.

Solomon was born in Israel in the tenth century BC, and was the son of David and Bathsheba. He had an elder brother, Adonias, David's son by Haggith, but David chose Solomon to succeed him as king, not only because Bathsheba pressed him to do so, but because he no doubt recognised Solomon's distinguishing quality as an administrator. Under Solomon's rule Israel reached the height of its fame. His territory which, for administrative purposes, he divided into twelve parts, extended from the River Euphrates to the border of Egypt. He held his kingdom together, and with his astute foreign policy, he made an alliance with Tyre and Egypt which enabled him to trade freely in the Mediterranean and south-east Asia. One of his most notable achievements was the building of the magnificent Temple at Jerusalem, which took seven years to complete. He also built fortified cities and splendid palaces. He was a magnificently attired king, and in riches and in wisdom outvied all the kings of the world. He had 1,400 chariots and 12,000 horsemen. He had 700 wives, each with the status of queen, and 300 concubines in his vast harems. But the taxes and forced labour he exacted from his people to run his extravagant court, his harems and his palaces, caused discontent. Some of his women enticed him to worship alien gods to whom he built shrines on the mountainside. This behaviour went against the charge his father David left him before he died, and 'brought the anger of the Lord upon him', and Solomon in his old age began to have enemies. Solomon reigned for forty years and when he died, about 933 BC, his kingdom was split in two—Israel and Judah. His son, Rehoboam, succeeded him as king of the smaller Judah. Jeroboam, a rebellious servant of Solomon's, succeeded as king of Israel.

Solomon's first wife was Pharoh's daughter, and among his concubines was the queen of Sheba whom he entertained lavishly. The glory of his reign is the source of many legends in the Talmud and the Koran, and Solomon himself was a prodigious author. Among the biblical writings attributed to him are the Song of Songs, Proverbs and Ecclesiastes. Perhaps the best-known example of his wisdom is the story of the two women who came to him with a live and a dead baby (related in I Kings iii: 16–28). Each woman claimed the live baby was hers. Solomon ordered that the child be cut in half and shared between them. One woman screamed and begged Solomon to give the whole child to the other woman rather than kill it. Solomon knew then that she was the true mother and ordered the child to be given to her. This kind of fair dealing is known as the Judgement of Solomon.

Lady Godiva

THE STORY OF LADY GODIVA riding naked through the streets of Coventry in the year 1040 is a well-known legend. But why she did it, in an age when women had to be almost hidden from society, is perhaps not so well known.

Lady Godiva, or Godgifu to give her her real name, was the wife of Leofric, Earl of Mercia, one of the powerful lords who ruled England under King Canute (see p80). Besides being beautiful, Godiva was very religious and charitable and cared much for Mercia and its people. Leofric, on the other hand, was a tyrant who cared for neither church nor people. He persecuted the church and imposed heavy taxes on the people of Coventry in order to help pay for the king's bodyguard. Godiva quarrelled frequently with her husband over his merciless behaviour and begged him to change his ways, and to be more lenient with the people.

During an argument one day, Leofric made the extravagant promise that he would remit the tax if Godiva would ride naked through the streets of Coventry on market day, knowing full well that this was something his pious wife would never do. But Leofric had forgotten Godiva's compassion and concern for the people. She mounted her horse and made her famous journey, clothed only by her beautiful long hair. Leofric kept his promise and the people of Coventry never again had to pay the taxes. Leofric also mended his ways and gave up persecuting the Church and tyrannising the people. He and Godiva made up their differences and together they founded a Benedictine monastery, where they were both eventually buried—Leofric in 1057 and Lady Godiva in 1085. But nothing remains today of the monastery.

The story of Lady Godiva was first recorded, in Latin, in the twelfth century by Roger of Wendover, a monk from St Alban's Abbey in Hertfordshire. He heard the tale from travellers resting at his abbey on their way to London. This story has been adapted by various historians and writers since, but there seems no reason to doubt that Lady Godiva did exist and did ride through the streets of Coventry. Some versions of the tale say that she rode through a crowded market place, others assert that the people stayed indoors behind shuttered windows, except one man—a tailor named Tom—who could not resist having a peep, and was immediately struck blind for his churlish action. He has ever since been known as 'Peeping Tom', a name as famous as Lady Godiva herself.

The Lady with the Lamp

God bless Miss Nightingale,
May she be free from strife;
These are the prayers
Of the poor soldier's wife.

TO THE THOUSANDS OF sick and wounded soldiers lying in the filthy conditions of the Crimean War, the Lady with the Lamp was a symbol of hope and comfort. Each night she walked the hospital wards where they lay and the soldiers touched her shadow as it fell across their beds, safe in the knowledge that she was there.

The Lady with the Lamp was Florence Nightingale, a Victorian socialite who forsook the comforts of life to become a nurse when nursing was a despised occupation followed only by the dregs of society. She was born in Florence—from whence came her name—on 12 May 1820 and was the daughter of Fanny and William Nightingale. As she grew up, she realised that the trivialities of an idle social life were not for her. To her mother's disappointment she had no inclination for marriage. She was lonely and unhappy and not having much in common with her elder sister, she had no one to confide in. But she poured her inner thoughts into what she called 'private notes', and all through her life she recorded her true feelings, writing on any scrap of paper that came to hand. In one of these notes she recorded: 'On February 7, 1837, God spoke to me and called me to his service.' She was not sure what form this service was to take. She knew only that the high society she was thrust into was not for her. As the years went by the desire to become a nurse formed in her mind; but no lady ever became a nurse and she knew the task would be difficult. Her obsession grew to such proportions that her parents arranged for her to travel with friends to Italy and Egypt in the hope of distracting her mind. But Florence used her travels to learn about nursing and eventually arranged to train with Pastor Fliedner's deaconesses at Kaiserwerth in Germany. She then went to Paris to work with the Sisters of St Vincent de Paul, but fate was against her and she was called home to help nurse her dying grandmother. By now Florence's family were beginning to accept that she was destined to become a nurse. She rejected the social whirl in which she shone; she spurned the love and offer of marriage from 'the man I adored', and forsook the family she loved, especially her valetudinous elder sister, who was so dependent on her. In 1853, at the age of thirty-three, she was selected to be the Superintendent of the 'Establishment of Gentlewomen during Illness' in London's Harley Street. When her family heard the news, her mother almost fainted and had to be given sal volatile, her sister had to be put to bed, and her father went to find solace in his club—but he relented so far as to make her an allowance of £500 a year.

Florence's nursing career had really begun. The following year the Crimean War broke out and for the first time ever a war correspondent, William Howard Russell of *The Times*, sent back despatches of the soldiers' sufferings. The country was appalled to learn of the way the sick and wounded were treated. The French had their Sisters of Charity to help them and they also had plenty of surgeons and adequate medical arrangements. Angry letters to *The Times* demanded to know why British soldiers were not so cared for. The Army was furious at the newspaper's interference and refused to admit that the soldiers were neglected. But still the storm raged and on 15 October 1854 Sidney Herbert, the Secretary at War, wrote to Florence Nightingale asking if she would go out to Turkey to organise the nursing. She accepted without hesitation. She gathered a party of thirty-eight nurses and on Saturday 21 October she left London for Scutari.

Her work in the Crimea was not easy. Conditions were appalling, the military authorities were suspicious and resentful of her, supplies were short and the nurses were disobedient and quarrelsome. But

Florence introduced discipline and order. She insisted on improved sanitation and adequate supplies, and by careful nursing saved the lives of many soldiers. In gratitude the soldiers refrained from swearing and coarseness in the presence of the nurses. Besides nursing the soldiers she encouraged them to write home to their families, and she herself wrote hundreds of letters to the families of the soldiers who died. At night, when the wards were quiet, she would do her rounds with her lamp, making sure that all was well. The soldiers loved her and she soon became a legend as 'the Lady with the Lamp'.

After the evacuation of the British Army from Turkey in 1856, she returned to England, exhausted and weakened by her arduous task. As a tribute to her work in the Crimea a public subscription was opened, and with the money raised she opened a school of nursing at St Thomas' Hospital in London, in the summer of 1860. Her health was not strong enough for her to take charge of the training school herself, but for years she continued to work for the cause of nursing. She spent the last years of her life at her home in South Street, London, never leaving her bedroom after 1896. By 1901 she had become completely blind, but still her spirit was undaunted. The legend of Florence Nightingale continued to grow. In November 1907 King Edward VII awarded her the Order of Merit—the first time it had ever been given to a woman—and the following year she received the Freedom of the City of London. She died on 13 August 1910, aged ninety. In accordance with her wishes her funeral was simple, and six army sergeants carried her coffin to the family grave at East Wellow in Hampshire. Her memorial is a simple inscription on the family tombstone: 'F.N. Born 1820. Died 1910.'

La Traviata

THE HEROINE OF VERDI'S romantic opera, *La Traviata*, was inspired by a little French waif, Rose Alphonsine Plessis, who became a famous Parisian courtesan.

Rose was born in 1824 in the tiny French village of Nonant, near Bayeux in Normandy. She was an unhappy little girl and at thirteen she ran away from home to live in Paris. She had no money and in order to buy food she turned to prostitution. So that her family could not trace her and take her back home she changed her name to Marie Duplessis. She was a captivating beauty and by the time she was eighteen she had become a famous courtesan. She lived on Paris's fashionable Boulevard de la Madeleine, and was visited by many rich socialities.

One day, as she was stepping out of a carriage on the Place de la Bourse, she was spotted by the younger Alexandre Dumas. He thought her exquisitely beautiful and when he saw her again, sitting in a box at the Variety Theatre, he asked a friend to arrange an introduction, and so began a lifelong romance. Marie, who suffered from chronic tuberculosis, told Dumas that he would have a sorry mistress, 'a woman who is nervous, ill, sad, and gay with a gaiety sadder than grief, a woman who spits blood and spends 100,000 francs a year. All the young lovers I have had have very soon left me.' But Dumas loved her dearly and would not be put off. As her illness worsened, he spent all his money paying for doctors and eventually bankrupted himself. He never deserted her, even when she married an old flame, Vicomte de Perregaux.

Marie died on 3 February 1846 before she had reached her twenty-second birthday. She was buried in the cemetery at Montmartre in a coffin that was covered with camellias, her favourite flowers. Dumas was heartbroken and soon after her death he wrote his novel, based on her life, *La Dame Aux Camélias*, which was first published in 1848. Later he turned the novel into a play, which inspired Verdi's opera, *La Traviata*—The Lady Gone Astray—which was first produced at the Teatro la Fenice in Venice in March 1853. In a very few years she had come a long way fom the street urchin of Nonant.

Lawrence of Arabia

THOMAS EDWARD LAWRENCE BECAME known as the legendary Lawrence of Arabia after he had successfully led an Arab revolt against the Turks during World War I.

Lawrence, who was born at Tremadoc in Wales on 15 August 1888, won an exhibition to Jesus College, Oxford, and whilst an undergraduate, in the summer of 1909, tramped through Syria to study the crusaders' castles and search for Hittite remains. After gaining a first-class degree in history, he was awarded a four-year travelling scholarship and in 1911 joined an expedition excavating the ruins at Carchemish. When the dig ended he travelled through Mesopotamia, Palestine, Egypt, Asia Minor and Greece. His companions were natives and he paid his way by doing local jobs such as camel-driving, harvesting and coaling ships. This way he really got to know the Arabs and was trusted and befriended by them.

In January 1914 he went with a party, under the leadership of Colonel S. F. Newcombe of the Royal Engineers, to make a survey of the Sinai peninsula. At the outbreak of World War I, he was employed at the War Office to make a map of Sinai. When war was declared against Turkey on 5 November 1914, Lawrence was sent, as a colonel, with Newcombe and others to form a Middle East intelligence service in Egypt, and to help the emir, Husein, who was trying to induce the Arabs to revolt against the Turks. Lawrence was the moving spirit in this successful turning point in the Middle Eastern theatre of the war. He organised and led raids on the Damascus to Medina railway, captured various vital posts and fought his way through Palestine to reach Damascus at the same time as the British.

After the war he attended the peace conference at Versailles, wearing Arab dress, but was bitterly disappointed that he could not gain satisfaction for the Arab demands. He refused a Victoria Cross and a knighthood that was offered him, declaring that he did not wish to profit from his championship of the Arabs, and withdrew from public life to write his account of the revolt—*The Seven Pillars of Wisdom* which was published in 1926. In 1919 he accepted a fellowship of All Souls, Oxford and in February 1921 became Middle East political adviser to the Colonial Office.

Towards the latter half of 1922, Lawrence changed his name to J. H. Ross and enlisted in the Royal Air Force. The following February his disguise was discovered and he was discharged. But within a month, he changed his name again, to T. E. Shaw, and enlisted in the Tank Corps. In August 1925 he was given a transfer to the RAF and sixteen months later was sent to the North-West Frontier in India, where he remained until the beginning of 1929. Again his disguise was becoming suspect and reports of supposed recognition came from places as diverse as Hong Kong, Ankara, and Tibet. But Lawrence managed to survive recognition and arrived back in England, where he worked on motor-boat construction and speed trials for the RAF at Plymouth and on the Solent until his discharge in February 1935. On 13 May he was flung over the handlebars of his motorbike while trying to avoid two pedal cyclists not far from Bovington Camp in Dorset, and died in hospital six days later.

Lewis Carroll

WE USUALLY THINK OF Lewis Carroll simply as the author of the nonsense books, *Alice in Wonderland* and *Alice Through the Looking Glass*. But Lewis Carroll was the pen name of a brilliant mathematician named Charles Lutwidge Dodgson.

Dodgson, who was born in 1832, was educated at Rugby and Oxford. After graduating in 1855 he became a lecturer in mathematics at Christ Church College, Oxford. Six years later he was ordained deacon, but he chose not to become a priest because of his natural shyness and a stammer. His shyness also prevented him from making friends easily and he resorted to the company of little girls, particularly the daughters of the Dean of Christ Church, with whom he felt at ease. It was for one of these daughters, Alice Liddell, that he wrote his famous Alice books. The books, which were illustrated by John Tenniel, a *Punch* cartoonist, became popular with adults as well as children, and the intellectual quality of the 'nonsense', which logically points out the absurdities of life, have kept them alive as perennial masterpieces.

Besides his nonsense books and poems, Dodgson, who was said to be a rather boring mathematical lecturer, wrote serious books on Euclidian geometry and formal logic. But valuable though these were, they did not enjoy the immortality of his less serious works.

Dodgson died in 1898, aged sixty-six.

Little Jack Horner

Little Jack Horner sat in a corner
Eating his Christmas pie,
He put in his thumb, and pulled out a plum
And said, 'What a good boy am I'.

THE PLUM IN THE nursery rhyme was not of the fruit variety, and the Christmas pie was not really for eating.

According to legend, little Jack Horner was the steward to Richard Whiting, Abbot of Glastonbury Abbey in Somerset at the time of the Dissolution of the Monasteries in the 1530s. Apparently the Abbot, in an attempt to make peace with Henry VIII, decided to send the king the deeds of twelve manors which belonged to Glastonbury. For safety's sake, the deeds were hidden in a huge pie, which was entrusted to Jack Horner to take to London to present to His Majesty. The trusted steward knew what was in the pie, of course, and on the journey, when he was safely out of sight of his master, he managed to carefully lift the crust and 'pull out a plum', which was the deeds of the Manor of Mells in Somerset.

Whether this story is true or not will never really be known, but the nursery rhyme lives on. And although a Jack Horner has not been traced as the owner of the Manor of Mells, it is certain that a Thomas Horner once owned it.

Lord Haw-Haw

LORD HAW-HAW WAS AN Irish American who broadcast anti-British propaganda in English from Nazi Germany during World War II. His real name was William Joyce and his nickname was given to him by a Fleet Street journalist because of the sneering, plum-in-mouth way he used to talk when delivering his propaganda speeches, which always began, 'Germany calling, Germany calling'.

The son of an Irish-American citizen, he was born in New York City, USA, on 24 April 1906, but lived most of his life in England and Ireland. Before World War II he was an active member of Sir Oswald Mosley's Fascist movement, and a co-founder of the National Socialist League. In 1938 he obtained a British passport, having stated falsely that he was born in Ireland and so a British subject. In August 1939 he went to Germany and joined Josef Goebbels' propaganda ministry.

All through the war he interrupted British radio with his propaganda speeches, but his broadcasts were regarded with amusement by the British people, rather than fear.

When the war with Germany ended in May 1945, Joyce was arrested and tried for treason. Although he was not a British subject, counsel for the prosecution maintained that since he was in possession of a British passport he owed allegiance to Britain. He was found guilty and, despite appeals for clemency to the House of Lords, was hanged on 3 January 1946.

Lucrezia Borgia

LUCREZIA BORGIA, THE ILLEGITIMATE daughter of Rodrigo Borgia (Pope Alexander VI) and sister of Cesare (see p35), was one of the most notorious women in history. She was beautiful, with fair hair and blue eyes, and her father and brother used her as a pawn in their merciless political manœuvres.

Lucrezia was born in 1480 of the same mother as Cesare and was her father's favourite daughter. She grew up, the centre of attraction, in the luxury and pomp of the papal court, and became the undisputed mistress of the Vatican while Rodrigo reigned as Pope. She was surrounded by vice, violence and intrigue, and although she was high-spirited and determined she reacted passively to the marriages arranged for her by her father to further the interests of the Borgias.

She was married three times. First, after two broken engagements, in 1493 to Giovanni Sforza of Pesaro. This marriage was annulled four years later after Giovanni accused Lucrezia of incest with her father. Pedro Calderon, the Pope's chamberlain, then became her lover and was consequently murdered. In 1498 Lucrezia gave birth to a son. Whether the father of the child was Calderon or Lucrezia's brother Cesare, is a matter for conjecture. Later that year she married Alfonso of Aragon, Duke of Bisceglie, to whom she was devoted. Two years later, Cesare, jealous of the young couple's influences over his father, had Alfonso murdered. In 1501 Lucrezia became regent while her father visited his Papal States, then later that year she married her third and final husband, Alfonso d'Este, heir to the Duke of Ferrara. In the peace and quiet of the Este court she reformed and despite a couple of love affairs with Francesco Gonzaga, Marquis of Mantua and the poet Pietro Bembo, lived an exemplary life. She devoted herself to good works and became a patron of the arts. She was an excellent wife and mother and her praises were sung throughout Ferrara. As Duchess of Ferrara, which she became in 1504, she lived on, free from vice and intrigue long after the reign of the Borgias had ended in Italy, and died in 1519.

Machiavelli

Am I politic? am I subtle?
Am I a Machiavel?

THE WORD MACHIAVELLIAN, meaning cunning and unprincipled, comes from the name of the Florentine statesman and writer, Nicolo Machiavelli, author of the controversial political treatise, *The Prince*.

Nicolo di Bernardo dei Machiavelli was born of a distinguished family in Florence on 3 May 1469. He served as envoy for the Florentine Republic, undertaking important diplomatic missions which gave him an insight into the squabbles and intrigues of Italian politics and brought him into contact with unscrupulous powerful figures such as Cesare Borgia (see p35).

Machiavelli was a brilliant man, but equally cunning and unscrupulous. He maintained that government authority should be established by any means, evil or otherwise. He believed in the divine right of rulers and his doctrine influenced many monarchs throughout Europe for many years. His ideal of a ruler was an absolute tyrant.

When the Medicis returned to rule Florence in 1512, Machiavelli lost his office. Soon afterwards he was accused of being part of an abortive conspiracy against the Medicis and was imprisoned and tortured. He was released a few months later by Giovanni de Medici, who ruled as Pope Leo X, and retired to his estate at San Casciano, near Florence. Here he devoted himself to reading politics and writing.

The constant warfare in Italy during the Renaissance induced him to write his famous book *Il Principe*—The Prince—which he dedicated to the younger Lorenzo de Medici, in whom Machiavelli saw a potential saviour of Italy. In the book, whose chief character of the Prince was modelled on Cesare Borgia, Machiavelli advocated that only a powerful, ruthless prince could reinstate order and free Italy from foreigners. The purpose of the book was to show Lorenzo de Medici how useful Machiavelli could be to him as a political adviser. Whether the book ever reached Lorenzo, or whether he ever read it, is not known, but he certainly never gave Machiavelli employment.

Machiavelli continued to write and became a popular figure in Florentine literary society. In 1520, Cardinal Giulio de Medici, who later ruled as Pope Clement VII, commissioned him to write the *History of Florence*. This took him until 1525 to write, just as the reign of the

Medicis was coming to an end. In 1526 Florence threw off the yoke of the Medicis and they were once more banished from power. Machiavelli was away from Florence at the time, but hurried back in the hope of securing employment again under the new Republic, but because of his associations with the Medicis he was not reinstated in his old office. He was then taken ill and died on 22 June 1527, at the age of fifty-eight. It is not known where he is buried, but there is a memorial to him, alongside other famous Florentines in Santa Croce, Florence.

Madame de Pompadour

OF ALL THE BEAUTIFUL mistresses that Louis XV of France gathered about him, the most powerful was the vivacious, red-headed Madame de Pompadour.

Her name was Jeanne Antoinette Poisson and she was born in Paris in 1721 of lower middle-class parents. She began her climb to fame when her father fled abroad for eight years to escape creditors. Her mother found a rich guardian who gave Jeanne an expensive education and arranged for her to marry his nephew, Guillaume Le Normant. As a hostess Jeanne began to attract much attention. She had an instinctive taste for gracious living and could sing, act and hold an intelligent, animated conversation with her intellectual guests, among whom were Voltaire and Quesnay. She caught the eye of Louis XV at a masked ball at the Palace of Versailles in the spring of 1745 and left her husband to become Louis' mistress. The following summer he created her Marquise de Pompadour and presented her to the queen, so establishing her at court as his mistress.

Because of her humble origins she was resented at court, but she soon overcame this obstacle and acquired great influence, which she held for more than twenty years. Louis was a feckless king who was always looking for change and amusement and his mistress saw that he got it. She introduced a theatre into court, the *Théâtre des Petits Cabinets*, which staged 122 different plays, operas and ballets in five years, with Madame de Pompadour always playing the leading lady. Her idea started a fashion for privately owned theatres in large country houses. She inspired the king with her passion for all the arts and paid huge sums of money for artists to decorate the many beautiful houses and gardens which the king had given her. Her influence and patronage of the arts was of great importance. She helped many artists and writers and founded the Sèvres china factory, in which she always took a personal interest.

Despite her complete influence over the king , she generally confined her political interference to internal affairs such as appointing ministers. Yet she is thought to have inspired a change of alliance which involved France in the Seven Years War.

Madame de Pompadour ceased to be Louis' mistress after 1751, but remained a close friend and adviser. Her hectic life at court seems to have shortened her life, for she died in 1764, at the age of forty-three.

Madame de Pompadour was followed as favourite mistress by Marie Bécu, a shop assistant, who became Madame du Barry. She tried to carry on Madame de Pompadour's patronage of the arts but she did not have the same influence as her predecessor. When Louis XV died she was forced into retirement by Louis XVI. In 1792, at the height of the French Revolution, she was guillotined for treason.

Madame Tussaud

THE FAMOUS WAXWORKS MUSEUM in London, which schoolboys usually call Madam Two Swords, is one of the country's most famous attractions. But few know the history of the little lady who created the vast exhibition.

Madame Tussaud was born Marie Grosholtz in Berne, Switzerland, in 1760. As a young girl she lived in Paris with her uncle, Dr Christopher Curtius, who taught her the art of wax modelling. When he died in 1793, Marie inherited his collection. She became art teacher to Louis XVI's sister, but at the outbreak of the French Revolution in 1789, she was imprisoned as a royalist. While in prison, she was given the job of making death-masks of heads freshly severed by the guillotine. This was a particularly unpleasant task for her as many of the victims were her friends.

After her release from prison in 1795, alone and friendless, she married François Tussaud, a French soldier, by whom she had two children. But the marriage was not a happy one and five years later they separated. In 1802, accompanied by her two small sons, Marie sailed for England, taking the contents of her museum with her. She exhibited the collection at London's Lyceum Theatre until December 1803, then began a successful touring exhibition of Britain, which lasted for thirty years. She finally opened a museum in London's Baker Street in 1834. When she died in 1850 aged ninety, she left the museum to her two children, who moved it to its present site in Marylebone Road in 1884. In 1925 it was destroyed by fire, but was rebuilt and reopened in 1928.

The museum contains some 500 life-size models of historical and present-day celebrities. Among the exhibits are some of Madame Tussaud's own works, including Marie Antionette, Louis XVI and Napoleon. In the Chamber of Horrors are some of the original French Revolution death-masks, the knife of the guillotine used during the Reign of Terror, and the key to the Bastille, the storming of which marked the beginning of violence in the Revolution.

Marco Polo

MARCO POLO WAS A Venetian traveller and adventurer who wrote the earliest known European account of the wonders of Asia after he had travelled overland to the court of Kublai Khan. A few months before Marco was born in 1254, his father and uncle left Venice to trade in the East. Their travels took them to China and the court of Kublai Khan where they were welcomed and fêted as they were the first Europeans the great Khan had met. Kublai Khan was interested in Christianity, and saw in it a means of opening up his vast empire to European culture and trade. He suggested that the Polo brothers should act as his ambassadors to the Pope with a request to send a hundred learned men to teach at the Khan's court. The brothers willingly agreed and were given safe conduct for their journey home. They arrived back in Venice in 1269. When Marco heard the magnificent tales his father and uncle had to tell of their travels he asked to be allowed to join them on their return journey to the great Khan's court.

Two years later, in 1271, the Polos set out again, taking seventeen-year-old Marco with them. They were also accompanied by two Dominican friars, sent by the Pope to instruct the Khan's court. The request for a hundred scholars could not be fulfilled, as none was prepared to make the hazardous journey. The friars abandoned their mission and turned back, leaving the three Polos to venture on alone. They journeyed on through Persia, Khurasan and the upper Oxus valley, over the Pamirs, through the Gobi Desert, and on via Suchow, Kanchow and Ch'angan, until in 1275 they reached Shangtu, in the extreme north of China, where the great Khan was at his summer residence. They had travelled thousands of miles on foot, through hazardous weather and often appalling conditions, suffering hardship and illness on the way. The great Khan welcomed them even more royally than before. He took a particular liking to young Marco, and took him into his service.

Marco learned several of the native languages and was sent on missions to various parts of the Khan's dominions, including Tibet, Burma, China and southern India. All the time he made notes of his journeys, recording the state of the cities and the people.

The Polos became very rich and after seventeen years they decided it was time to return home. Kublai Khan reluctantly agreed to let them go. He showered them with a fortune of gifts and jewels and early in

1292 they sailed from Chuanchow, taking with them a Mongolian princess who they were escorting to Persia for her wedding. After a long journey via the Strait of Malacca and southern India they reached Persia in 1294. The Polos continued their homeward journey and arrived back in Venice in 1295, quite unrecognised by their family.

Venice was at war with Genoa and the rich Polos equipped a galley which Marco commanded. He was captured in 1298 during the Battle of Curzola and imprisoned for a year in Genoa, where he wrote his famous book on his travels.

After his release from prison, he returned to Venice but little is known of his life afterwards. He died in 1324 and is buried in the Church of San Lorenzo in Venice.

Maria Marten

MARIA MARTEN WAS AN ordinary village girl who was murdered by her lover but her fame has lived on for almost two centuries.

Maria was born in 1801 in Polstead, Suffolk, and was the daughter of John Marten, a mole-catcher. Her mother died when she was a child and she was brought up by her father and a loving step-mother. By the time she was twenty-four she had had two illegitimate children—one by the squire's son who paid her generously for the child's maintenance. She then fell in love with William Corder, the son of a rich farmer. By him she had a third child, but it died when it was two months old.

William now wanted to end their relationship as his family disapproved of his association with Maria. He schemingly proposed marriage and Maria accepted. William then suggested that she should dress as a boy to accompany him as far as Ipswich, so as to avoid local gossip. Maria happily agreed and on a night in May 1827, she left the thatched cottage where she lived and made her way to the Red Barn, half a mile along the road, to change her clothing. William was there waiting for her. He cold-bloodedly shot her in the eye and stabbed her several times, then buried her under a bay of the barn.

William Corder pretended that all was well and wrote several letters to Maria's family, which purported to come from the Isle of Wight, telling them that he and Maria were married and were happy and prospering. But Maria's step-mother was suspicious about her step-daughter's absence and lack of direct communication. One day she told her husband that she had dreamed for three nights running that Maria had been murdered and was buried beneath the Red Barn. Her husband then went to the barn, and digging where his wife had indicated, he found the body of his daughter. A search was then launched for William Corder. He was found in Brentford, Middlesex, happily married to one of fifty girls who had answered his advertisement in a lonely-hearts column. He was convicted of murder, found guilty, and hanged at Bury St Edmunds, Suffolk, in August 1828. His trial had provoked public outrage, and after his execution, the hangman is said to have sold the rope at a guinea an inch. The prison surgeon flayed his body, and a copy of the account of the trial was bound in his skin. This, together with his skull, is kept in Bury Museum.

Maria's body was buried in Polstead Churchyard, but souvenir hunters long ago chipped away her gravestone. A melodrama, based on the story of the lovers, is still performed in Polstead.

Maria Montessori

MARIA MONTESSORI, WHO WAS born in Rome in 1870, was the first woman to receive a medical degree at Rome University. While working as a doctor in a mental institution in Rome she developed a method of teaching mentally backward children to read and write, which she later extended for use with normal children.

Maria believed that children could educate themselves if they were given the freedom to do so. Her teaching endeavoured to develop a child's initiative by allowing the child to perform tasks naturally and without conventional rules or rigid discipline. Her first success with normal children was in the slums of Rome where, in 1907, she opened the first of her *caso dei bambini*—children's homes.

The Montessori method of teaching, which soon spread beyond the Italian capital, is explained in Maria's own books. *The Montessori Method* describes teaching 3-6 year olds, and *The Advanced Montessori Method* develops the method for 6-10 year olds. An analysis of her method is found in *The Secret of Childhood*.

Maria died in 1952, but her teaching method is still influential.

Mata Hari

MATA HARI, AN ORIENTAL name meaning Eye of the Day, was the pseudonym of Margaretha Geertruida Zella, a Dutch dancer.

Margaretha, who was born in 1876, was married to a Dutch Army officer named Macleod, but after only a few years of marriage, she sought fame and fortune and left him to become a courtesan and oriental dancer in Paris. She adopted the intriguing name of Mata Hari, and being a very exotic-looking woman, soon became the confidante of men in high places.

In 1907, she joined the German Secret Service and during World War I she betrayed the many important military secrets that had been confided to her by the dozens of high-ranking allied officers who had fallen in love with her.

Although she worked for both the Germans and the French, the French arrested her in 1917. She was convicted of treason, found guilty and executed by firing squad.

Mona Lisa

WHO IS THE LADY known as 'La Gioconda' who smiles down enigmat-
ically on visitors who admire her in the Louvre Art Gallery in Paris?

Contary to popular legend, she apparently is not Mona Lisa. She is
thought to be Constanza d'Avalos, mistress of Guiliano de Medici,
youngest son of Lorenzo de Medici, the great Florentine ruler.

In 1503, Leonardo da Vinci was commissioned to paint a portrait of
Mona Lisa de Giocondo, the wife of a Florentine nobleman, who at
the time was mourning the death of her baby daughter. Her husband
thought it would help her grief if she sat for a portrait. It took Leonardo
four years to finish the painting and eventually he gave it to the
Giocondos. A few years later, Leonardo was asked by Guiliano de
Medici to paint a portrait of his favourite mistress, Constanza
d'Avalos. Strangely enough, Constanza looked rather like Mona Lisa
although she was nineteen years older, and even more strangely, she
was nicknamed La Gioconda—the smiler. Leonardo, as was often his
habit, had made two versions of his Mona Lisa, so he adapted his
other version, changing only the face to look like Constanza. But by
the time the painting was finished, Guiliano had given up his mistress
and settled down in marriage, and did not want to buy the portrait.
Leonardo then packed it up with his other unsold works and took it
to Paris, where he had been invited by King Francis I. And it is thought
that this is the painting known as the Mona Lisa which hangs in the
Louvre.

The original Mona Lisa remained with the Giocondo family until
early this century, when it found its way to England and was bought
first by an art museum in Bath and then by a Swiss syndicate, and now
hangs in the home of one of the syndicate members in London.

Mother Shipton

ONE OF THE BEST-KNOWN prophets of all time, Mother Shipton is said to have foretold the deaths of Cardinal Wolsey, Thomas Cromwell and Lord Percy, and prophesied the English Civil War, the Great Fire of London, the coming of railways and aeroplanes, the invention of telegraph and, like many others before and after her, the end of the world.

She was born Ursula Southeil, in a cave at Knaresborough, Yorkshire, in 1488. Her mother died giving birth to her, and Ursula was brought up by a woman who lived in a cottage in Knaresborough. As she grew up, strange happenings began to take place in the cottage— furniture moved of its own accord and food vanished from the plates at mealtimes.

When she was twenty-four, Ursula married Toby Shipton. Soon afterwards she became known as a fortune-teller and was called Mother Shipton. She was a big woman with a crooked body and an ugly face, but had an extraordinary perception and could well pass for a witch.

Her strange behaviour aroused the curiosity of her neighbours and they were always spying on her and prying into her private affairs. Mother Shipton is said to have got her own back by putting a spell on a party at which many of the neighbours were present. The guests all broke into uncontrollable laughter and ran from the house, each of them followed by a frightful looking goblin. The terrified neighbours told their story to the local magistrates, who then summoned Mother Shipton to court. She told the magistrates that far worse things would happen if she was not left alone. She then shrieked a curse at the magistrates 'Updraxi, call Stygician Helluei', and was then, according to reports at the time, carried away by something resembling a winged dragon. This could have been a wheeled sleigh pulled by a deer, since this was said to be Mother Shipton's favourite way of travelling.

Many of the prophecies attributed to Mother Shipton are now thought to have been invented by Richard Head, a publisher who brought out a *Life and Death of Mother Shipton* in 1677, and Charles Hindley who brought out a revised edition in 1862. But true, or false, Mother Shipton lives on in the folklore of England.

Mrs Moore

Don't have any more, Mrs Moore
Or you'll have to take the flat next door....

SO WROTE ARTHUR LECLERQ, the popular song- and scriptwriter in 1913. But Mrs Moore was not a figment of the songwriter's imagination—she was in fact the sister of Arthur LeClerq (pronounced L'Clare), and he wrote the song about her after she had had her seventh child.

Mrs Moore was born Georgina Mary Ann Howard on 17 December 1877, in Brixton, south London, and was the daughter of Georgie Wright, a principal dancer, and Charlie Williams, a music hall artiste—the pseudonyms of the Hon Mr and Mrs Charles Thomas Howard who were disinherited for going on the stage. On 9 May 1899, against her mother's wish, she married Roderick John Moore, an actuary, and a year later began to produce the children who were to send her into legend: Frances, Daisy, Roderick, Gertrude, McKenzie, Laurence, and Bernard. Mrs Moore then heeded her brother's advice. Three of the children died: Frances and McKenzie in childhood, and Bernard in 1932 when he was eighteen.

Mrs Moore, known to her family as Little Georgie, for she stood no more than 5ft high, was widowed in the early twenties and spent the rest of her life with her daughter Daisy and her husband George Hellicar and their family at Mitcham in Surrey.

A fun-loving, aristocratic lady with a ready wit and a fine tale to tell, she charmed old and young alike, and was an exciting, doting grandmother to her many grandchildren (of whom the author is one) and great-grandchildren. She died after a stroke on the morning of Corpus Christi, 13 June 1963 aged eighty-five, and is buried at Mitcham in the grave with her son, Bernard.

Mrs Moore's mother, Georgie Wright, made theatre history when she appeared as Flirt in *A Trip to Chinatown* at Toole's Theatre in the Strand, London, in 1894, and her name was put up in lights outside the theatre. This was the first time ever that lights had been used to display a star's name.

Muhammad

If the mountain will not come to Muhammad,
Muhammad must go to the mountain.

MUHAMMAD, AN ARABIC WORD meaning 'the Praised One', was the title-name adopted by the founder of the Islamic religion. His real name was Kotham, or Halabi, and he belonged to the Tribe of Koreish.

The son of a poor merchant, he was born in Mecca in AD 570. Both his parents had died by the time he was six and he was brought up first by his grandfather and then by his uncle. He started his working life as a shepherd until he married Kadija, a rich widow, and became a merchant like his father, only much richer. Kadija, who had been married twice before, remained his only wife for twenty-five years. It was a particularly happy marriage. After her death he married many others, nine of whom survived him.

Muhammad was a deeply religious man and often used to go alone to Mount Hira to meditate and pray. When he was forty years of age, he began to have visions and these continued for the rest of his life. In one revelation, in a cave on Mount Hira in 610, the Archangel Gabriel commanded him to start a new religion. Muhammad then began to preach in Mecca. He had a few followers, but mostly the Meccans resented him setting himself up as a reformer and prophet, and they objected to his preaching on the unity of God, the inevitability of judgement and the futility of worshipping idols. Muhammad persevered, but persecution became so unbearable that on 16 July 622 he and his followers fled Mecca for Medina, more than 200 miles to the north. This flight is called the 'Hegira' and the Muhammadan calendar starts from this event.

Muhammad gathered a band of Bedouin tribesmen about him and for eight years they campaigned relentlessly against the Meccans. Eventually, in 630 the Meccans capitulated and Muhammad returned to Mecca, unchallenged as prophet and leader of the new religion. Other Arab tribes joined his followers and the expansion of Islam began. Once the Arabs asked Muhammad for divine proof of his teaching. He then ordered Mount Safa to come to him. When it did not move, he explained that God was merciful, for had the mountain obeyed his command it would have fallen on to them and destroyed them. 'I will therefore go to the mountain and thank God that He has had mercy on an obstinate generation.' From this story comes the above phrase, which is often used to describe a person who, not being able to get his own way, accepts the inevitable.

Most of what is known about the life of Muhammad is contained in the *Koran*, the sacred book of his teachings, and the *Hadith*, a supplement to the Koran, containing stories about the prophet. Muhammad died in 632 at Medina, where he is buried.

Nostradamus

As good a prophet as Nostradamus

LIKE MOTHER SHIPTON (see p107), who flourished about thirty years before him, Nostradamus was a celebrated prophet of the sixteenth century.

Michel de Notre Dame, to give him his real name, was born on 14 December 1503, at St Remy in Provence, France, and was brought up as a Roman Catholic by converted Jewish parents. He studied philosophy and medicine and graduated as a doctor at Montpellier University in 1529. He became famous as a doctor during an outbreak of the plague when his skill and devotion saved many victims from death, no doubt because of his refusal to bleed them—a controversial step in the sixteenth century. Nostradamus was controversial in other ways, too. He believed, a hundred years before Galileo, that the earth went round the sun, and in 1547 he began to make prophecies. But how he regarded his claims himself is not possible to say.

His prophecies, all couched in ambiguous language, were written in verse form and divided into centuries. He published them in a series of books entitled, simply, *Centuries*. The first seven appeared in 1555. The second edition contained ten centuries and was published in 1558. At the time, astrology was in fashion and his books were a success. Catherine de Medici invited him to visit her, the Duke and Duchess of Savoy went to see him, and when Charles IX became King of France, he appointed Nostradamus his physician-in-ordinary.

Nostradamus made no secret of his fortune-telling. Just as a gypsy gazes into a crystal ball, he gazed into a bowl of water placed on a brass tripod. But sometimes his predictions happened spontaneously, as when he was travelling in Italy one day, he knelt before a passing Franciscan Friar and, to the Friar's astonishment, said: 'I kneel before His Holiness.' In 1585 the Franciscan became Pope Sixtus V, one of the greatest popes.

Nostradamus, who latinised his name early in his career, died on 2 July 1566. In 1781, his *Centuries* were formally condemned by the Papal Court. Because of their ambiguity they gave rise to much speculation as to their authenticity, but some theories maintained that Nostradamus wrote in such a bewildering way to avoid being accused of witchcraft by the Inquisition. Many interpretations were put upon their meaning, and their obscurity gave rise to the phrase 'as good a prophet as Nostradamus', meaning so obscure that you cannot be understood.

Among the prophecies interpreted from Nostradamus's verses were the accidental death of Henry II of France in 1559, the Great Fire of London and the Plague, the rise of Napoleon, the Spanish Civil War, the abdication of Edward VIII, the rise of Hitler, V-bombs and the bombing of Hiroshima and Nagasaki. For the future he predicts the coming of a third anti-Christ (the first two were Napoleon and Hitler), who will emerge in China, and a war between China and a Russia–America alliance at the turn of the century.

Old Uncle Tom Cobbleigh

For I want for to go to Widecombe Fair
Wi' Bill Brewer, Jan Stewer, Peter Gurney,
Peter Davy, Dan'l Whiddon, Harry Hawk,
Old Uncle Tom Cobbleigh and all,
Old Uncle Tom Cobbleigh and all.

IT IS NOT KNOWN who wanted to borrow Tom Pearce's grey mare to go to Widecombe Fair with all his friends. Nor is it known who the friends were, except Old Uncle Tom Cobbleigh—and he really did exist.

In the Devonshire village of Spreyton, twelve miles north of Widecombe in the Moor, there lived a farming family named Cobbleigh. One of the farmers was a bachelor called Tom, and he is the likely character immortalised in the famous song.

As a young man Tom was wild and amorous. He also had bright red hair and this characteristic, which was no doubt blamed for his hot-headedness, also spared him having to pay countless sums of money in paternity orders which were constantly being issued against him, for he refused to maintain any child that did not have red hair like himself.

Tom died in 1794 and is buried in Spreyton churchyard in an unmarked grave. There is a tombstone marked Thomas Cobbleigh outside the south porch of the church, but this belongs to Uncle Tom's nephew.

A plaque depicting the story of Uncle Tom and his friends on the grey mare can be seen on the village green at Widecombe. And each year when Widecombe Fair is held in September, an 'Uncle Tom Cobbleigh' rides in on a grey mare. The original grey mare which 'took sick and died' after carrying such a load such a long way, is said to haunt the moor: 'When the wind whistles cold on the moor of a night, Tom Pearce's old mare doth appear gashly white, wi' Bill Brewer, Jan Stewer, Peter Gurney, Peter Davy, Dan'l Whiddon, Harry Hawk, Old Uncle Tom Cobbleigh and all, old Uncle Tom Cobbleigh and all.'

The Old Woman Who Lived in a Shoe

There was an old woman who lived in a shoe
She had so many children she didn't know what to do

IN 1682 A YOUNG woman named Elizabeth Foster married a widower named Isaac Goose in Boston, Massachusetts, USA, and immediately became the step-mother of ten children. Within a few years she had produced six children of her own. Two died in infancy, but Mrs Goose was still left with fourteen children.

Fortunately Mrs Goose was a great story-teller and had a fund of fairy tales and nursery rhymes which she related to her family to keep them amused. Some of the stories she knew from her own childhood, others she made up as she went along, and the one shown above is very likely one of the latter—a tale about herself.

Luckily for Mrs Goose one of her daughters married a printer named Thomas Fleet and he gathered all his mother-in-law's tales together and printed them in a book entitled *Songs for the Nursery*. No known copy seems to have survived, but research shows that the American Mrs Goose may have contributed to the Mother Goose nursery rhymes that we know today.

Mrs Goose died in 1757 and is buried in the Old Granary Burial Grounds in Boston.

Paul Revere

Listen, my children, and you shall hear
Of the midnight ride of Paul Revere

LIKE DICK TURPIN (see p40), Paul Revere is renowned mainly for a famous ride. But there the resemblance ends, for while Turpin was galloping to save his own neck, Paul Revere was racing to warn fellow Americans that the British troops were going to arrest them and seize the ammunition they intended to use in the first battle of the War of Independence.

Paul, who was born in Boston, Massachusetts, on 1 January 1735, was the son of a Huguenot immigrant. He was a creative, versatile young man and with his father he learned to work silver. By his mid-twenties he was producing some of America's most beautiful pieces, but he also found time for politics, becoming a Son of Liberty in 1765. He took part in the Boston Tea Party in 1773, and later became the official courier for the Massachusetts provincial assembly. When the Boston safety committee learned that Britain's General Gage was going to attack the colonists' supply depot and arrest the revolutionary leaders, they sent Paul Revere to warn the countryside. He sped off and rode the sixteen miles from Boston to Lexington in two hours, enabling the revolutionary leaders Samuel Adams and John Hancock to escape and the colonists to move their ammunition to Concord, five miles away. The following day, 19 April 1775, the American War of Independence began.

Paul did great service during the war, printing banknotes and man-ufacturing gunpowder. But he was disappointed that his main task, commanding a fort at Boston, was not an active one. Then he took part in the Penobscot expedition of 1779. This ended in retreat and Paul was accused of cowardice. He never again sought the glory of leadership, but three years later he obtained a court-martial which declared him innocent and cleared his name. After the war he went back to his job as a craftsman. As well as fashioning silver, he started a copper and brass foundry, and this factory supplied sheet copper sheaths for American ships during the War of 1812.

Revere maintained his interest in politics and was a staunch sup-porter of the new constitution. He died in the city in which he was born, Boston, Massachusetts, on 10 May 1818. He is immortalised in Longfellow's poem *The Midnight Ride of Paul Revere*.

Pocahontas

The blessed Pocahontas,
as the historian calls her,
And great King's daughter of Virginia.

POCAHONTAS WAS A YOUNG Red Indian Princess who saved the life of one British colonist and brought peace between the British and the Algonquin Indians of Virginia, when she married another.

She was the daughter of Chief Powhattan, head of the Algonquin Indians in Virginia, USA. When she was born in 1595 she was given the personal name of Matoaka, but her father nicknamed her Pocahontas, meaning playful, pet child.

When she was twelve years old, the British, led by Captain John Smith, landed in Chesapeake Bay and began to colonise Jamestown. Pocahontas became friendly with the colonists and when Smith, who had been captured by the Indians, was about to be executed, she flung herself down, took Smith's head in her arms and successfully begged her father to spare him. The following year, 1609, Smith returned to England. Relations between the white men and the Indians deteriorated still further, and on 13 April 1613 Pocahontas was kidnapped by the colonists and held as security for the English prisoners taken by Powhattan. She was treated kindly by the colonists during her captivity and was taught English, converted to Christianity and baptised Lady Rebecca by the Reverend Alexander Whitaker, a voluntary missionary in Virginia.

Eventually, in 1614, Pocahontas was ransomed by her father, but by then she and John Rolfe, one of the colonists, had fallen in love. Both Chief Powhattan and Thomas Dale, the Governor of Virginia, agreed to their marrying and peace was firmly established between the Indians and the colonists. The following year Pocahontas had a son, Thomas, and on 21 April 1616, the Rolfes came to England.

Pocahontas was a huge success. She was lionised by English society who accepted her as a princess, and was presented at the court of James I. While she was in England, Pocahontas met John Smith, whom she had been led to believe was dead. Smith knew she was a married woman with a son, and refused to see her again. Pocahontas enjoyed England and did not want to return to Virginia, but Rolfe was adamant about returning. They boarded a boat on the Thames near Woolwich Reach. Pocahontas was far from well, but her husband assured her the sea journey would cure her ailment. She became gradually worse, and as the boat reached Gravesend she was taken ashore and rushed to a wharf-side inn, where she died a few minutes later of smallpox. She is buried beneath the chancel in St George's Church, Gravesend.

John Rolfe returned to Jamestown a few weeks later, but their son, Thomas, was left at Plymouth in the care of Sir Lewis Stukely. Thomas returned to Virginia in 1635, when he was twenty. About 1644 he married Jane Poythress, the daughter of a landowner. They had a daughter, Jane, the first of Pocahontas's many descendants.

Pretty Witty Nell

'A BOLD MERRY SLUT', Samuel Pepys, the diarist, called her, but slut or not, Nell Gwynne, Pretty Witty Nell, rose from selling oranges in London's Drury Lane to be favourite mistress of Charles II, so ensuring herself a place in history.

She was born on 2 February 1650 and her accepted birthplace was Pipe Well Lane, Hereford, now renamed Gwynne Street after her. Some sources claim that she was born in Coal Yard, off Drury Lane, where her father was a fruiterer. As a young girl she sold oranges from the pit of the Theatre Royal in Drury Lane and soon caught the attention of the actors. She went from the pit to the stage at the age of fifteen and was given her first stage part as Cydaria in Dryden's *Indian Emperor*. More parts followed and she was soon accepted as an outstanding comedienne. She was short and plump-cheeked, but her long reddish-brown ringlets, shapely legs, and wild, saucy personality charmed all the fashionable young men of the day. 'Pretty witty Nell', wrote Pepys in his diary, 'beyond imitation almost.' 'The indiscreetest and wildest creature that ever was in a court', said Bishop Gilbert Burnet.

Her chief success was in reciting prologues and epilogues, many of which Dryden wrote especially for her. Standing on stage one night, in a hat 'of the circumference of a large coachwheel', reciting one of her saucier pieces, her fate was sealed. She looked so droll that Charles II could not resist her. He took her home in his coach to supper and she became his mistress. From then on she called him Charles III as she had already had two lovers named Charles. She bore him two children, Charles Beauclerk who was later made the Duke of St Albans, and James who died when he was nine.

Her popularity as the king's mistress was enhanced by the people's dislike of her main rival, the Duchess of Portsmouth. Once, while driving to Oxford in the king's retinue, her coach was jostled by a mob who thought it contained the Catholic duchess. Nell Gwynne put her head out of the window and delighted the crowd when she shouted: 'Pray, good people, be civil. I am the protestant whore.'

Charles II never lost his affection for Nell, though according to Burnet, 'he never treated her with the decencies of a mistress'. His other mistresses had all been made duchesses. But she was always 'Nelly' to him, for just as she was to be created Countess of Greenwich the king died. On his deathbed, Charles implored his brother, James II, 'Let not poor Nelly starve', the words as famous as Nell Gwynne herself. James heeded his brother's dying wish and Nell Gwynne's debts were paid, and a large sum of money and an estate in Nottingham were settled on her. She died suddenly of a stroke on 13 November 1687, outliving the king by almost three years. She is buried in the Church of St Martin-in-the-Fields, London, in the same tomb as her mother.

Rasputin

GREGORI YEFIMOVICH RASPUTIN WAS a Russian adventurer and monk, who wielded much influence at the court of Tsar Nicholas II and the Tsarina Alexandra.

He was born in 1871 at Pokrovskoye in Siberia, and was the son of a poor peasant. Although he was married with a family, his dissolute way of life earned him the name by which he has always been known—Rasputin, meaning debauchee. He was influenced by a fanatical sect called the Khlysts, who believed that the way to salvation was through sin and repentance. Rasputin claimed further that part of the Deity was within him and that physical contact with him would bring purification. This doctrine led to wild orgies, but in the remote part of Siberia where he lived he was regarded as a holy man.

During a pilgrimage to Kiev, Rasputin met the Grand-Duchess Militsa, who introduced him into high places and eventually to the Tsarina, whose son, the Tsarevich Alexis, suffered gravely from haemophilia. Doctors had failed to help the boy, but Alexis often improved after Rasputin's intervention. Alexandra soon came to regard Rasputin as a spiritual comforter as well as a saviour to her son.

Rasputin grew more powerful at court and he was soon having a say in ecclesiastical affairs as well as politics and matters of state. Indignation against him in court and public circles grew, but Alexandra would listen to nothing bad about her holy man of God, as she called him. She was completely under the influence of the monk whose jet-black hair and near-set eyes gave him the look of a maniac. Damage was being done to the royal family's reputation because of her association with him and towards the end of 1916 a plot was formed by three young nobles to kill him. On the night of 30 December, he was assassinated and his body thrown into the River Neva. When she learned what had happened the distraught Empress had his body buried in a special chapel at Tsarskoye Selo, which she visited every night for spiritual comfort.

St George

Thou Saint George shalt calléd be,
Saint George of merry England, the sign of victory.

ALTHOUGH THE STORY OF St George killing the dragon may be only a legend depicting the triumph of the Christian hero over evil, St George himself did exist. He was an officer in the army of the Roman emperor, Diocletian, and was martyred by Diocletian at Nicomedia, on 23 April 303, for refusing to persecute Christians when the emperor began his terrible ten-year purge against them.

The legend about the dragon was told by the Dominican friar, Jacobus de Voragine, in his *Golden Legends,* written in Latin in the thirteenth century and translated and published by William Caxton in 1483. But the martyrdom of St George has been known in England since about the eighth century. The Venerable Bede (see p148) mentioned him in his *Martyrology* and Aelfric, the scholar-clergyman, also wrote about him in the tenth century. But his popularity dates from the year 1098 when he came to the aid of the first Crusaders at the siege of Antioch. By then he had become the patron of soldiers, and in a later Crusade, Richard the Lion Heart (Richard I) placed himself and his army under his protection. In 1348 Edward III founded the Most Noble Order of the Garter under his patronage. He became accepted as the patron saint of England after Henry V's order before the Battle of Agincourt, 'Forward banner, in the name of Mary and St George', better known in Shakespeare's words: 'Cry God for Harry, England and St George.'

St George was undoubtedly recognised as the personification of Christian chivalry. Besides being the patron saint of England he was adopted as patron by Venice, Genoa, Portugal and Catalonia. Numerous churches have been named after him, and countless paintings and sculptures have been made of his image.

In England, the emblematic symbol for St George is the red rose— a rose being the Christian symbol for a paragon.

St James the Great

ST JAMES, THE BROTHER of St John and the son of Zebedee, was the first apostle to die for the Christian faith. He was beheaded by the sword of King Herod Agrippa in Palestine in AD 44.

According to legend, after his death his followers put his body in a marble coffin which they launched upon the sea. It was eventually washed up at Cape Finisterre on the north-west coast of Spain, where, again according to legend, St James is said to have first preached the gospel. It lay hidden for almost 800 years, until in AD 840 the people of Finisterre saw strange lights in the sky and heard angels singing. They told their bishop, Thedemirus of Iria, and he, led by a star, found the coffin containing a skeleton, which divine revelation told him was the remains of St James. The bishop had the coffin taken inland to a field, which was later named *La Compostela*—the field of the star. The villagers built a shrine around the coffin, and pilgrims gathered there to pray for help in the fight for Spain against the Moors.

Eventually a small church took the place of the rude shrine and then, in the eleventh to thirteenth centuries the present magnificent Roman-esque cathedral was built.

St James, who was one of the three apostles to witness the Trans-figuration and the Agony in the Garden of Gethsemane, was adopted as the patron saint of Spain and accepted as the defender of Christianity against the Moors.

St Patrick

Oh St Patrick was a gentleman
Who came of decent people;
He built a church in Dublin town,
And on it put a steeple.

THE ABSENCE OF SNAKES in Ireland is said to be due to St Patrick, who is supposed to have chased them all out in the fifth century.

Strange as it may seem, St Patrick, the apostle of Ireland, was not an Irishman. He was born in Dumbarton, Scotland, about AD 373 and was the son of Calpurnius, a Roman official. When he was about sixteen Patrick, whose name was then Sucat, meaning warlike, was captured during a Pictish raid and sold as a slave to Miliuc, a chief from County Antrim. For six years he worked as a stockman, then at the age of twenty-two he escaped to Gaul where he studied under St Martin at Tours and was ordained priest. He then returned to his parents in Britain, but soon had a calling to return to Ireland to preach to the heathens. Despite parental opposition, he set off on his mission and landed at Wicklow on the east coast. His reception was rather discouraging so he sailed round the coast to Strangford Lough, where a chief lent him the use of a barn. And so began his conversion of Ireland: first Ulster and then the rest of the country. He eventually established his headquarters at Armagh and his fervour and enthusiasm gained him many followers. After its conversion, Ireland became a centre of Christian influence in Europe.

St Patrick founded many churches and monasteries, and many have since been named after him. He is usually depicted with a shamrock leaf as tradition says that when he was explaining the Trinity to the heathens at Tara he used the leaf as a symbol. Although Patrick was never formally canonised in Rome, he is accepted as a saint by popular tradition. More about St Patrick can be learned from his autobiographical *Confession* and his *Epistle to Coroticus*. He apparently died in 461, although other dates have been given, and various places claim to be the site of his death and burial. His feast day is kept on 17 March.

St Simeon

I, Simeon of the pillar, by surname
Stylites, among men; I Simeon,
The watcher on the column till the end....

SIMEON STYLITES WAS THE first of a class of Christian ascetics who lived on the tops of pillars in order to lead holy and solitary lives and who became known by his surname. The Stylites, or Pillar Saints as they were sometimes called, were found mainly in Syria, where they originated, but also in Mesopotamia, Egypt and Greece, during the fifth to twelfth centuries.

Simeon, who was born about AD 390 in Cilicia, Syria, became a hermit in Antioch. His strict principles won him a group of followers and he later retired to the platform of a pillar, which over the years he gradually increased to a height of 72ft. There he spent thirty years in contemplation and preaching to the pilgrims who, attracted by his saintliness, had gathered below. Many people were converted to his way of life and many imitated him on the tops of pillars. His most famous follower was St Daniel, who spent thirty-three years on a pillar in Constantinople. St Simeon died in 459.

The Stylites never descended from their pillars. They lived standing up and leant against the wall for their short bouts of sleep. Their scanty food was taken up to them by their disciples or sent up in a basket.

The life of St Simeon fascinated the poet Tennyson who wrote a poem about him entitled *St Simeon Stylites*.

Santa Claus

SANTA CLAUS OR TO give him his real name, St Nicholas, was a Bishop of Myra in the fourth century. Like St George (see p123) he is venerated in both eastern and western Christianity. He is said to have been made a saint on the strength of one miracle—rescuing three generals from being unjustly executed by the Emperor Constantine. Another miracle attributed to him was the resurrection of three little boys who had been murdered, cut up and put into a pickling tub to be served as bacon. He is also said to have tossed gold into the homes of penniless girls so that they did not have to earn their dowries in a disreputable way.

St Nicholas's fame spread quickly throughout the Byzantine and Roman empires, but his immense popularity stems from 1087 when merchants from Bari in southern Italy rescued his relics from the Turkish Seljuks advancing on Myra and took them back to Bari, where they now lie in the Church of St Nicholas.

St Nicholas is the patron saint of Russia, Aberdeen, pawnbrokers, clerks, scholars, children and sailors. The pawnbroker's three gold balls are said to represent the three bags of gold he tossed into the homes of the poor girls. His popular name of Santa Claus is a corruption of the Dutch name, Santa Nikolaus. His feast day is 6 December, and in some countries Christmas presents are distributed on the night of 5 December. The custom used to be for someone to dress as a bishop and give small gifts to children who had been good. The present custom of putting toys and other small presents into a stocking on Christmas Eve was introduced into Britain from Germany in 1840.

Savonarola

GIROLAMO SAVONAROLA WAS AN Italian Dominican friar, who waged
a one-man crusade against the tyranny and corruption of Florence in
the fifteenth century and was executed for doing so.

The son of a court physician, he was born at Ferrara in 1452 and
studied the humanities, philosophy and medicine before joining the
Dominican order in 1474. From an early age he was deeply concerned
about the worldliness of the Florentines and determined to stir their
consciences to repentance. He was a highly emotional preacher, and
his political skill, humour, and prophetic inspiration won him vast
popular support. Year after year, people flocked to the cathedral to
hear his fiery Lenten sermons, even although they were always on the
same theme—the need for reform in society and the church. He bitterly
criticised the immorality of Pope Alexander VI and prophesied the
punishment of the Church and Italy.

For three years after the downfall of the Medicis, he virtually ruled
Florence, persuading the citizens to heed his prophecy and turn from
their wayward habits. Then in 1495, the Pope ordered Savonarola to
Rome to justify his claim to divine revelation, but he refused to go,
claiming ill-health and fear of violence on the way. 'It is not the will
of God that I leave Florence', he told the Pope. The Pope then ordered
him to stop preaching and when he refused to do so the Pope ex-
communicated him. The Pope also threatened to ban worship in
Florence unless the city could silence Savonarola and make him ask
for absolution.

Florence then became divided between supporters and opponents of
Savonarola until his popularity waned and he was handed over to the
Papal commissioners for trial. He was tortured and found guilty of
heresy and handed back to the civil authorities for sentence. On 23
May 1498 he was hanged and his body burned.

Florence had lost one of its greatest teachers and Savonarola, the
victim of a vicious political system, died because he believed in his
individual thought and his power to interpret God's will.

Simon Bolivar

SIMON BOLIVAR WAS A Venezuelan revolutionary leader who was in-strumental in freeing much of South America from Spanish rule. So fine a soldier was he, and so great were his victories, that in his early days he was known as the Napoleon of South America. In his later days, when his liberating policies were accomplished, he became known as the Washington of his people, for having devoted his life to liberty.

Bolivar, who was a member of a rich, aristocratic Basque family which had moved to Venezuela in 1578, was born in Caracas on 24 July 1783. After an initial private education at home, he travelled to Europe where he absorbed the ideas of thinkers such as John Locke and Spinoza and the great French Enlightenment philosophers. The seeds of liberation began to germinate in Simon during a visit to Paris in 1804 when he was inspired by the patriotism of Napoleon, who then declared himself Emperor of France. But it was in Rome, the following year, standing on the Aventine Hill, that he vowed to liberate his country from Spanish domination.

He returned to Caracas in February 1807 and the following year plunged into the separatist movement which had been precipitated by Napoleon's invasion of Spain. He became its leader in 1813. Undeterred by early setbacks, he fought on, but his attempts at revolt were unsuc-cessful and he was driven out of Venezuela and Colombia by the royalists and fled to Jamaica. But Bolivar was a stalwart and did not give up. He returned to South America and in the following years of relentless campaigning he freed first Colombia at the Battle of Boyaca and then Venezuela at the Battle of Carabobo. Next he liberated Ecuador and finally Peru.

Bolivar, who had become the first President of Gran Colombia (a union of Venezuela, Colombia and Ecuador), became dictator of Peru, the southern region of which had been renamed Bolivia in his honour.

His last years were spent in disappointment and poverty, precipi-tated by the disputes between his former associates. Gran Colombia was split up again, and an attempt was made on his life in Bogotá. He died at the early age of forty-seven on 17 December 1830, near Santa Marta, Colombia.

Sir Cloudesley Shovell

ADMIRAL SIR CLOUDESLEY SHOVELL was a poor boy from a Norfolk fishing village who left his job as apprentice shoemaker to go to sea, and rose from cabin boy to Rear-Admiral by virtue of his remarkable ability and outstanding courage. He died in a shipwreck off the Scilly Isles, at the age of fifty-seven.

In 1674, while serving as a lieutenant in the Mediterranean, he burned four pirate ships off Tripoli. In 1689 he commanded a ship at the Battle of Bantry Bay and was later knighted for his conduct. He took active part in many more sea battles and in January 1705 he was made Rear-Admiral of England. Two years later, in 1707, he commanded his ship HMS *Association* during the capture of Barcelona, but was unsuccessful with his attack on Toulon.

On the way home his ship struck a rock off the Scilly Isles on the foggy night on 22 October 1707 and sank with the loss of 800 men, including Sir Cloudesley. Three other ships of his fleet also struck the rocks with the loss of more than 2,000 men.

Sir Cloudesley's body was washed ashore the next day and he was buried in Westminster Abbey.

According to legend, a sailor aboard Sir Cloudesley Shovell's ship knew the waters well and hastened to warn Sir Cloudesley that the fleet was heading in the fog for the dangerous Gilstone Reef. The indignant admiral ordered the sailor to be hanged for his impertinence. As the rope was put around the sailor's neck he put a curse on Sir Cloudesley by reciting Psalm 109, 'Let his children be fatherless and his wife a widow', which according to old superstitition was the cursing psalm. When Sir Cloudesley's body was washed ashore at Porth Hellick Cove on St Mary's he was still alive. An old woman found him and hacked off his fingers so as to steal his rings. She then buried him alive on the beach. On her deathbed she confessed the crime and a monument now marks the spot where the body was found.

Sir Francis Dashwood

SIR FRANCIS DASHWOOD IS perhaps best known as a practical joker and founder of the Hell-fire Club—a club for reckless, irreverent young men who mocked religion and practised black magic. But despite his love of practical jokes, he did have a serious side to his nature, which is all too often overlooked.

In 1724, when he was sixteen, he succeeded his father as 2nd Baronet. Then, like most aristocrats of that time, he set out on a grand tour of France, Italy and Germany. Three years after his return he set out again, and altogether made six grand tours of the Continent. But it is said that Francis was more interested in adventure than furthering his education.

When he finally settled in England he became a member of the Prince of Wales's set and of the Tory opposition party, known as the King's Friends. From this political clique, about 1755, he formed his Society of St Francis of Wycombe, more commonly known as the Hell-fire Club or the Monks of Medmenham. He limited membership to twenty-four young men of high social standing, and among those who belonged were the Earl of Sandwich, John Wilkes and the poet Paul Whitehead. The Club's motto was *Fay ce que voudras*, 'do what you will', and the 'Monks' held black masses and mock religious ceremonies in the ruined Cistercian Abbey at Medmenham, which formed part of the Dashwood estate. They also held orgies and black magic rituals in caves which Sir Francis had had cut into the hillside opposite his home of West Wycombe Park in Buckinghamshire. The Hell-fire Club broke up in 1763, when Dashwood let loose a baboon as Lord Sandwich was conducting a ceremony invoking the devil. The members thought the devil had appeared and fled in terror. Dashwood was never forgiven.

Because of his legendary Hell-fire Club, Sir Francis's serious activities tend to get forgotten. But he was a founder member of the Dilettanti Society and a fellow of both the Royal Society and the Society of Antiquaries. He received an Honorary Doctorate of Law at Oxford and served as Chancellor of the Exchequer from 1762 to 1763, and joint Postmaster-General from 1766 until his death in 1781. Benjamin Franklin, the American scientist, who often stayed at West Wycombe with him, described Dashwood as the best company he knew.

In 1762 Sir Francis's uncle, the Earl of Westmorland, died, and left him a great deal more land and the barony of le Despencer, and from then on he became known as Lord le Despencer.

Despite his weird sense of humour and highly intelligent but facetious conversation, he was a caring man. With Benjamin Franklin he produced a shortened version of the Book of Common Prayer designed to help old and sick people who could not 'remain for hours in a cold church'. It was later used as the basis of the American Episcopalian prayer book. He also led an unsuccessful campaign in 1757 to save Admiral Byng from being shot, as a scapegoat for the loss of Minorca during the Seven Years War.

Dashwood died in 1781, aged seventy-three, and his epitaph read: 'Revered, Respected and Beloved by all who knew him.'

Sir Philip Sydney

SIR PHILIP SIDNEY, POET, scholar and one of the most admired of Elizabeth I's courtiers, was regarded as the perfect example of an English gentleman.

He was born at Penshurst Place in Kent on 30 November 1554, and after an education at Shrewsbury and Christ Church, Oxford, travelled extensively on the Continent. He was in Paris during the Massacre of St Bartholomew and sought refuge with the English Ambassador, Sir Francis Walsingham, whose daughter he eventually married.

Philip's uncle was the Earl of Leicester, Queen Elizabeth I's favourite, and this connection opened the doors of court to him. When it was proposed that Elizabeth should marry the Duke of Anjou, Leicester, fearing that his personal position would be threatened, induced Sidney to write a letter advising the Queen against such a marriage, as Protestantism, which she favoured, would be threatened. Elizabeth took exception to the advice and Sidney retired from court for a while and went to stay with his sister, the Countess of Pembroke, at Wilton.

During this time, much of his literary work was produced. His collection of sonnets, *Astrophel and Stella*, was the first and finest of the Elizabethan sonnet sequences. Astrophel was a pun on his own name. Phil Sid, a diminutive of Philip Sidney, was also a diminutive of *Philos*

Sidus. The Latin *sidus* was changed to the Greek word *astron*, making astron-philos—star lover. The star, or stella, was Penelope Devereux, whom Sidney admired at the time. Another 'invention' of Sidney's was the name Pamela, probably from the Greek words *pan*, meaning all, and *melos*, tune, which he used for a character in his chivalric romance, *Arcadia*. Again, *Arcadia* developed a literary style, and his *Defence of Poesie* was the most eloquent and critical essay of the Elizabethan period.

In 1583 Sidney returned to court and was knighted. He was married in the same year. In 1586 he went with Leicester to the Low Countries to support the Dutch against the Spanish occupying forces. During a raid on Zutphen, Sidney's thigh was shattered by a musket ball. He rode from the battle-scene and was about to drink from his water-flask when he saw a dying foot soldier. Sidney handed the parched soldier the flask, saying: 'Thy necessity is greater than mine', an action which won him immortality. Sidney was taken to Arnhem, where he died from gangrene on 17 October 1586. In February 1587 he was buried in St Paul's Cathedral. He was mourned throughout the nation for he had been regarded as the embodiment of chivalry and virtue, and his noble action in the face of death set the seal to his reputation.

Sir Roger Tichborne

SIR ROGER CHARLES DOUGHTY TICHBORNE was the twenty-five-year-old heir to the ancient baronetcy of Tichborne in Hampshire and an officer in the Sixth Dragoons. When his love affair with his cousin Katherine ended in March 1854, he resigned his commission and sailed for Valparaiso to forget her. After travelling for a month in South America, he boarded the sailing ship *Bella* at Rio de Janeiro, bound for Jamaica. But the ship went down and nothing more was seen or heard of Roger Tichborne.

His French-born mother, Henriette, refused to believe that he was dead, and after the death of her husband, Sir James Tichborne, in 1865, she advertised in newspapers in South America and Australia, offering a reward for information about her son. One of these advertisements was seen by Arthur Orton, a poor working-class man from Wapping in London's East End, who was working as a cattle-slaughterer in Wagga-Wagga under the assumed name of Tom Castro. Orton, who was about to file a bankruptcy claim, decided to 'confess' to his solicitor that he was the owner of property in England. He also dropped a hint that he had been shipwrecked. He then began carving the initials RCT on trees and fences. His solicitor, who had also seen the advertisements, became suspicious and asked him outright if he was Roger Tichborne. Orton admitted he was and his solicitor persuaded him to write to Lady Tichborne about his 'inheritance'.

In 1866 the imposter sailed for England with his wife and child. They landed on Christmas Day and Orton immediately went to Hampshire to make himself known among his 'home surroundings' before approaching Lady Tichborne. The Tichborne locals were horrified at his claim. Sir Roger, when he left, was a slim, cultured young man, with straight black hair. Orton was coarse, had fair wavy hair and weighed 24 stone. 'If you are Sir Roger', the village blacksmith told him, 'you have changed from a racehorse to a carthorse.' But Orton decided to go ahead with his fraudulent claim.

Orton met Lady Tichborne and the grief-stricken old woman, who had waited eleven years for the return of her son, believed that a miracle had happened and that he had returned from the dead. Despite the difference in appearance, she professed to recognise him and made him an allowance of £1,000 a year. The rest of the family were not deceived and would have nothing to do with Orton.

Safe in the knowledge that his 'mother' recognised him, Orton began legal proceedings to claim the Tichborne estates from the trustees of the infant son of Sir Roger's deceased younger brother. Before the case was heard, Lady Tichborne died, and Orton lost his only supporter. Orton then gathered what evidence he could and when his case came before the court he had a hundred witnesses testifying that he was the real Sir Roger Tichborne, with only seventeen Tichborne witnesses testifying that he was not. The case lasted for 102 days and finally Orton's claim was found to be false and he was identified as Arthur Orton, son of a Wapping butcher. His course manner and rough way of speaking had condemned him. 'If only I could have kept my mouth shut, I would have won,' he said after the case. He was then sent for trial for perjury. This second case lasted 188 days, and ended with Orton being sent to prison for fourteen years.

Orton served ten years of the sentence and when he was released he tried, in vain, to regain public sympathy. He did various odd jobs, but poverty was catching up with him, so he sold his confession to the *People* newspaper for £3,000. When he died on 1 April 1898, one unknown supporter put an inscription on his grave which read: Sir Roger Charles Doughty Tichborne, born 5 January 1829, died 1 April 1898. And so ended the most famous case of impersonation in the history of English law.

Sir Thomas More

'Our sentence is that Thomas More shall be taken from this place by William Kingston, the Constable, to the Tower and thence shall be hanged, cut down while yet alive, ripped up ... his head cut off....

That brutal sentence was passed on sixteenth-century England's greatest scholar, and one of the liveliest minds in Henry VIII's court, because he refused to betray his conscience.

In his book *Utopia*, Thomas More described an imaginary land where wise, happy people live in harmony and where crime, poverty, injustice and other social ills do not exist. And although More managed to live his personal life among his family in this way, public life in Tudor England was a far cry from his Utopia.

More, who was born in London in 1478, had intended to become a priest, but gave up the idea to study law. Although he remained a devout Catholic, he was one of the leading lights in the 'new learning' of humanism. He was an intimate friend of Erasmus, John Colet and other humanists, and together they tried to reconcile traditional religion with the new science of humanism.

In 1504 he became a Member of Parliament and the same year married Jane Colt. He was a brilliant lawyer and, in 1518, successfully represented Pope Leo X in a civil action regarding the seizure of a ship. His skill so impressed Henry VIII that he was persuaded to relinquish his legal practice and was sworn in as privy councillor and made Master of Requests. In 1520 he accompanied Henry to the Field of the Cloth of Gold (a plain near Guines, France, where Henry met Francis I of France and so-called because of its spectacular pageantry). The following year he was knighted. A brilliant career in the royal service lay ahead of him. As well as his official duties he wrote poetry, books about English history and biographies. In 1529, after Cardinal Wolsey's downfall, he became Lord Chancellor of England. He established a reputation for hard work and integrity, but in 1532 he resigned his office because he could not accept Henry VIII's intention to divorce his first wife, Catherine of Aragon. More retired into private life to enjoy the company of his family. But Henry would not leave him in peace. He wanted support for his intention to gain supreme power over the Church as well as the state and for his intention to be rid of his wife, who could not produce the son and heir he so desperately wanted. In 1533 Henry married Anne Boleyn and More's absence from the coronation made him a marked man. Trumped-up charges of receiving bribes when he was chancellor were proved groundless, but in April 1534 he was ordered to swear the Oath of Supremacy. He agreed to swear the Oath of Succession declaring Anne Boleyn's daughter the rightful heir to the throne, but he could not and would not deny the Pope and swear the Oath of Supremacy declaring Henry head of the Church. He was cast into the Tower of London and despite desperate pleas from his favourite daughter, Margaret, to change his mind, stood by his resolution.

On 1 July 1535 More was taken to Westminster Hall for trial under a recently enacted Act for Treason. He knew what to expect of a Tudor state trial. All the usual exaggerated evidence, false accusations and perjured testimony were brought against him. Nothing could save him, but the King in his 'clemency' changed the sentence to one of simple beheading and on 6 July 1535 he was taken to Tower Hill and beheaded. His daughter Margaret saved his head from being thrown into the river and kept it reverently, despite demands from the King's Council to surrender it. When she died in 1544 the head was buried with her.

In 1886 More was beatified, and in 1935, four hundred years after his death, he was canonised by Pope Pius XI.

Socrates

SOCRATES WAS AN ANCIENT Greek philosopher who was sentenced to death at the age of almost seventy for allegedly corrupting the youth of Athens by his teaching. The death sentence, which was brought about by jealous fellow teachers, was unjust for all of Socrates's pupils, among whom were Plato and Euclid, maintained that Socrates believed emphatically in moral values, austere conduct of life and the unity of knowledge, wisdom and virtue. So upright was Socrates that although he could have escaped from prison on many occasions, he would not do so, despite pleas from his friends. He believed that man is bound by conscience to respect the law of the state, and so felt obliged to respect the sentence, even though he knew it was wrong. He died in prison by drinking hemlock in the presence of his grief-stricken followers.

Socrates, who was the son of a stonemason and a midwife, was born in 469 BC. He did not claim to be wise or to possess any knowledge. And when the Delphic Oracle was asked whether there was any man wiser than Socrates and it replied clearly and simply, and not in its usual obscure way, 'No one is wiser', Socrates was very disturbed. He claimed only that he was ignorant and was aware of his ignorance.

Before he began to teach, he had been a soldier in the Athenian army and distinguished himself on the battlefield. Later he became a member of the Athenian administration. But he did not need to work. He owned his own house in Athens and had a little money which one of his pupils, Crito, a city businessman, invested for him. So he could afford to teach without fees and it was this fact that aroused the jealousy of other teachers and made influential Athenian citizens suspicious of his motives. It did not help him that he would not suit his teaching to political party purposes. He was ugly, slovenly, eccentric and fond of jesting, but his pupils adored him. He did not put his teachings into writing and did not found any school of philosophy. He taught orally and most of his teaching has come down in history through his most important pupil, Plato. His method of teaching was by asking questions, while pretending to be ignorant, and drawing out the answer from the student. This method, known as maieutic, he likened to his mother's profession of midwifery, and he considered himself to be a midwife to men's thoughts. He believed that virtue is understanding and that no one wittingly does wrong. Cicero summed him up by saying, 'he brought down philosophy from the heavens to earth', and that he taught that 'the proper study of mankind is man'.

Sun Yat-sen

WANTED: Dead or Alive
Sun Yat-Sen
£100,000.

THE ABOVE NOTICE WAS issued in October 1896 by the Imperial Chinese Government in their attempt to capture the young man intent on organising London's exiled Chinese into a revolutionary movement.

Sun Yat-sen, who won fame as the father of the Chinese Republic, was born in 1866 and was the son of a poor Cantonese peasant. When he was thirteen he left home to join a much older brother who had emigrated to Hawaii and prospered. Whilst there Sun learned English and became a Christian. He then went to Hong Kong, where he studied medicine at the medical school set up by Sir James Cantile, a distinguished London surgeon and missionary. He graduated in 1892 and spent the next few years practising as a doctor in Macao and Canton. But Sun was disgusted by China's backwardness and the corrupt regime of the Manchu emperors and decided to devote his life to political revolution. He took part in a revolutionary coup. This failed and the conspirators were executed—except for Sun, who managed to escape. He fled to England to the safety of his old friend, Sir James Cantile.

Sun lodged at Gray's Inn Place, London, not far from Cantile's Devonshire Street home, and from there he began to organise London's Chinese population into his revolutionary movement and to circulate anti-Manchu propaganda wherever he could. Sun thought he was safe in London, but the displeased Chinese government demanded his capture, dead or alive, and put a price on his head. One Saturday morning, when London's fog was at its thickest, Sun was kidnapped by Chinese government agents and imprisoned in the Chinese Legation in Portland Place. Arrangements were made for him to be drugged and shipped back to China. 'We are not barbarians,' the Legation officials told him. 'The proper formalities will be observed. First the trial and then the beheading.' While he was awaiting transportation, he smuggled a letter through a guard to Sir James Cantile, who invoked the help of the Foreign Office and made the case known to the newspapers. A few days later Sun Yat-sen was released.

He continued to work for the freedom of China and in 1911 a revolt against the Manchu broke out in Hangkow. In February 1912, the

Manchu emperor abdicated and Sun Yat-sen was proclaimed provisional president of the Chinese Republic. He held the office for forty-five days, then for the sake of national unity, withdrew in favour of the northern general Yuan Shih-k'ai who had been elected Prime Minister of the national assembly in Peking. Yuan then became president of the republic, but during the next three years he abused his presidency and tried to become a dictator. Sun Yat-sen opposed his regime, as he had opposed the ways of the Manchus, but was defeated and exiled. In 1921 he was re-established as provisional president of the South China Republic. He was toppled from power by the war lords, but was re-elected at Canton in 1923. He then sought the help of the Russians to reorganise the Kuomintang (the Chinese Nationalist Party, which he founded) to admit communists.

Sun Yat-sen did not live long enough to see the fruits of his life's work. He died of cancer on 12 March 1925. His body was embalmed and laid in a temple near Peking. Four years later it was removed to a specially erected mausoleum at Nanking.

The Swedish Nightingale

THE GIRL WHO EARNED the nickname of the Swedish Nightingale was Jenny Lind, one of the most celebrated sopranos of all time.

She was born in Stockholm on 6 October 1820 and made her operatic début as Agatha in Weber's most famous opera *Der Freischutz* at the Stockholm opera house in 1838. She studied under Manuel Garcia in Paris, and then toured Europe before going to England where she eventually settled permanently in 1847. After distinguishing herself in opera in her early years, at the age of twenty-nine she turned to concert work and oratorio, and was introduced into America in 1850 by the impresario Phineas T. Barnum. In 1852 she married the German-born pianist and composer Otto Goldschmidt, who accompanied her at many of her concerts.

Frail and not much to look at, she seemed to light up when she sang. Her exquisite voice, pure and controlled, had a range between G and E. Audiences loved her and crowds used to stand outside her house in London begging her to sing. On three occasions the House of Commons was without a quorum because the Members had gone to the opera house to listen to her. She also won the lasting admiration of composers such as Mendelssohn, Chopin and the Schumanns. Clara Schumann said that her voice was 'all soul'.

At the age of sixty-three, she became a singing teacher at the Royal College of Music. She was very generous and endowed many charities and musical scholarships. She died at Malvern in Worcestershire on 2 November 1887, four weeks after her sixty-seventh birthday.

Tamburlaine

THE GREAT-GREAT-GRANDSON of Genghis Khan, Tamburlaine was one of the fiercest conquerors of the Middle Ages. He was born at Kesh, fifty miles south of Samarkand, in 1336. He usurped the throne of Samarkand at the age of thirty-three and then launched upon a series of brutal military campaigns which did not end until his death at the age of almost seventy.

He conquered Persia, Georgia, Armenia, Circassia, and the whole area between Khurassan and the Caspian Sea. He overran India and was proclaimed Emperor of Hindustan. He swept on to Syria, Damascus and Baghdad, and then headed for China. But his avarice was cut short at Otrar on 17 February 1405, when he died suddenly.

In war, Tamburlaine, which is a corruption of Timur i Leng or Timur the Lame, was a brutal, cold-blooded murderer of thousands of fellow human beings. He was ruthlessly deaf to any plea for mercy, so determined was he to regain the empire of his great-great-grandfather. But, mighty conqueror that he was, he was no administrator and he made no attempt to consolidate the vanquished countries into one empire. Conquest was enough for him. Yet it has been said that in peace he was kind and just, and fostered learning and the arts.

More about Tamburlaine, or Tamerlane as he is sometimes called, can be learned from the plays by Christopher Marlowe (*Tamburlaine the Great*, written in the sixteenth century), and Nicholas Rowe (*Tamerlane*, written in 1701).

Tannhäuser

TANNHÄUSER WAS A THIRTEENTH-CENTURY German minnesinger, or lyrical poet, who frequented the courts of the dukes of Austria and Bavaria. He led a wandering life and went on a crusade to the Holy Land. He is even believed to have visited the far east. But Tannhäuser is not remembered for his wanderings or for his amatory poems, but by a legend which sprung up about him in a sixteenth-century German ballad.

This tells how Tannhäuser, a worldly knight, discovers Venusberg, a sorceress's court reached by an underground cave in a magic mountain. There he spends a sensual year with the goddess Venus until, overcome by remorse at having sinned, he goes back to the upper world to seek absolution from the Pope. His Holiness tells him that he can hope for forgiveness as much as he can expect the Papal staff to break into blossom. Tannhäuser leaves the Pope in despair, but three days after his departure the Papal staff burst into bloom. The Pope sent messengers in every direction, but the despondent knight could not be found. Believing that he could not be forgiven he returned to the magic mountain to end his days with Venus.

This legend about Tannhäuser was the theme of Wagner's opera of the same name.

Till Eulenspiegel

TILL EULENSPIEGEL WAS A Bavarian peasant around whom grew a collection of tales about cruel practical jokes.

Till was born in Brunswick about the beginning of the fourteenth century. His parents were very poor and, according to legend, Till avenged his fellow peasants by playing cruel and often crude practical jokes upon the townsfolk who, he believed, regarded the peasants as inferior beings. With a combination of peasant shrewdness and pretended stupidity he outwitted tradesmen, particularly innkeepers, merchants, priests and noblemen.

Till, who is also known as Ulenspeighel, or Tyll Howleglas or Owlglass, died near Lübeck in 1350, but he was the hero of the peasants' stand against ill-treatment during the next century. A collection of some 1,500 jests and brutal tricks had been attributed to him, and the first written account of his legendary roguish doings was published in a low German *Volksbuch* in 1483, but this has not survived. A second collection was published in Strasbourg in 1515. This text has survived and there is a copy in the British Museum in London. The stories were soon translated into most of the European languages and provided the French with a new word for rogue, *espiegle*, and the German expression *Eulenspiegelei*.

Many versions of Till's exploits have been written over the years, including Richard Strauss's symphonic poem *Till Eulenspiegel's Merry Pranks* (1895).

Uncle Sam

I'm a real live nephew of my Uncle Sam,
Born on the fourth of July....

SURPRISINGLY, UNCLE SAM, THE caricature in the frock-coat who per-
sonifies the government of the United States of America, really had a
human original. He was Samuel Wilson, a government inspector
known affectionately as 'Uncle Sam'.

During the early nineteenth century, an American named Elbert
Anderson owned a small shop in Troy, New York. The shop was
looked after by Ebenezer Anderson, a cousin of Elbert's, and Ebenezer's
uncle, Samuel Wilson. On the front of the shop were painted Elbert
Anderson's initials followed by the letters U.S., meaning United States,
since Elbert was a great patriot.

Sam Wilson was asked one day by an employee what the initials
U.S. stood for. Wilson jokingly replied that they stood for Uncle Sam
who, of course, was himself. And this seemed reasonable enough since
he helped to run the shop. But his joke cottoned on, and it was not
long before 'Uncle Sam' became synonymous with 'United States' and
was accepted as the national figurehead. It was first used as a deroga-
tory nickname for the U.S. government by New Englanders opposed
to government policies during the War of 1812.

The Venerable Bede

ONCE THOUGHT OF CHIEFLY as a theologian, the Venerable Bede is now appreciated as one of the greatest historians, and is sometimes called 'the Father of English History'.

He was born at Wearmouth in Northumbria in AD 673. When he was seven his parents died and he was placed in the care of Abbot Benedict Biscop at Wearmouth. At the age of nine he went with Abbot Ceolfrith to the newly built monastery at Jarrow where he spent the rest of his life, becoming ordained deacon at the early age of eighteen and a monk at thirty, the earliest age allowed by canon law. Apart from a few visits to friends within the confines of Northumbria, he never left Jarrow. Legends that he accompanied his fellow monks to Rome in 701 have been authoritatively discounted.

Bede, also known as the Monk of Jarrow, devoted himself to his monastic duties, to studying scripture and to writing, and as he says in one of his works, his 'special delight was always to learn, to teach, and to write'. He knew Latin, Greek and Hebrew, and besides being an historian and biographer he was conversant with all the scholarship of his time—grammar, rhetoric, mathematics and physical science.

Among his 150 works, forty are still known and these include comments on the Bible, *Lives of the Abbots*, *Epistle to Egbert*, various hymns and what is considered his greatest work, the *Ecclesiastical History of the English People*, which is the chief source of early English history up to the year 731.

Bede died on Ascension Day, 25 May 735, singing the *Gloria Patri*—'Glory be to the Father and to the Son and to the Holy Ghost'. He knew that he was going to die and despite ill-health, forced himself to complete his translation of St John's Gospel, the last few sentences being written by a boy helper.

When Bede died St Boniface wrote: 'The candle of the Church, lit by the Holy Spirit, was extinguished.' His remains, which were removed from Jarrow to Durham in 1020, were removed again to Durham Cathedral in 1370 and now lie in the Galilee Chapel under the inscription:

> '*Haec sunt in fossa*
> *Bedæ venerabilis ossa.*'

> '*The bones in this grave*
> *are those of the Venerable Bede.*'

The Vicar of Bray

And this is the law I will maintain,
Until my dying day, Sir,
That whatsoever king shall reign,
I'll still be the Vicar of Bray, Sir.

THE TURNCOAT RENOWNED IN the famous ballad 'The Vicar of Bray' was the Reverend Simon Aleyn, who held the living of the thirteenth-century church at Bray in Berkshire from 1540 to 1588. So determined was his reverence to retain his incumbency during the religious turbulence following the accomplishment of the Reformation in England that he changed his faith to suit the religion of the reigning monarch.

During the reigns of Henry VIII and Edward VI he was Protestant. Then came the Catholic Bloody Mary (Mary I), and he became Catholic, and back he went to Protestant again when Elizabeth I became Queen. When he was reproached for his religious inconstancy, he maintained that he had always been constant in his resolve to remain the Vicar of Bray.

Although Simon Aleyn lived in the sixteenth century, the ballad suggests that the Vicar of Bray lived in 'Good King Charles's Golden Days' and was incumbent at Bray from the time of Charles II until the reign of Queen Anne. And there was a vicar during this time, Simon Symonds, who was reputed to be high church under Charles II, Catholic under James II and Protestant when William and Mary came to the throne. But nevertheless, the accepted Vicar of Bray, who gave his name to fickle-mindedness, was Simon Aleyn.

The Warrior Queen

When the British warrior queen,
Bleeding from the Roman rods,
Sought with an indignant mien,
Counsel of her country's gods

ONE OF THE FIRST, and bloodiest, rebellions in English history was led by a woman and surprisingly her male army did not object to her leading them. The warrior queen was Boudicca, wife of Prasutagus, king of the Iceni, a tribe living in East Anglia. She was a formidable woman and according to one Roman historian, terrifying in her appearance, with fierce eyes, a harsh voice and a mass of tawny hair falling to her hips.

When Prasutagus died in the year AD 60, the Romans, who had invaded Britain seventeen years earlier, seized his lands and sacked the royal palace. Prasutagus had willed his property jointly between Boudicca and the Roman Emperor Nero, in the hope that he could circumvent the law which demanded that property of kings without sons passed to Rome. But the Romans ignored his will. The legionaries scourged Boudicca for her opposition and raped her two daughters. The Iceni were outraged and Boudicca raised a revolt. The whole of East Anglia and south-east Britain rose up with her. Boudicca's timing was perfect since the Roman governor, Suetonius Paulinus, and his army were two days' march away in North Wales fighting the Druids. Boudicca's war chariot charged ahead and the rebels followed. They captured and burned the Roman strongholds of Camulodunum (Colchester), Londinium (London) and Verulamium (St Albans). More than 70,000 people—Romans and the British who befriended them—were savagely slaughtered. Boudicca would have no prisoners and no bargaining. Death was by sword, cross, gibbet or fire.

But Boudicca's triumph was short-lived. Her food supplies were dwindling and her undisciplined followers were disbanding into plundering mobs. Paulinus and his legions, back from Wales, met up with the British near Fenny Stratford in the south Midlands. Paulinus prepared for battle in a narrow valley. Boudicca urged her army on to revenge, and although her soldiers outnumbered the Romans three to one, the discipline of the Romans won the day. The British were annihilated: 80,000 were slain and a despairing Boudicca escaped to the woods and poisoned herself.

The warrior queen's rebellion, savage though it was, was not in vain, for although there was a short period of vengeance against the Iceni, the Roman Emperor Nero pardoned the vanquished tribesmen and a system of justice was introduced, which was to last for more than 300 years.

The events of Boudicca's rebellion were recorded by the first-century Roman historian, Tacitus, in his *Annals*. Because of an error in the first printed edition of the *Annals*, Boudicca was known for years as Boadicea. Boudicca was also the subject of poems by Cowper and Tennyson. A statue of her at the reins of her chariot is on Westminster Bridge, London.

F. W. Woolworth

MOST OF US, AT some time or other, have been into Woolworth's in the High Street, but few are aware that this great chain of stores was the brain child of one poor American young man.

Frank Winfield Woolworth was born in Rodman, New York, on 13 April 1852. When he left school he took a course at a business college and at the age of nineteen became a shop assistant in New York. He was not a very good salesman, but after clerking (as being a shop assistant is called in America) for almost ten years he persuaded his employers to let him try a new method of selling that he had heard of. His employers gave him the chance, so he set up a counter offering a variety of goods at one price only—five cents. A year later his company backed him in opening a five-cent-only store in Utica, New York. Unfortunately this was a failure and closed within three months. But Frank was tough-minded and persevering. He was convinced that the failure was due to not enough variety in the goods, so the company agreed to back him again in another venture. This time he opened a five-and-ten cent store in Lancaster, Pennsylvania. Fortunately, this was successful and further stores were opened in other cities in New York, New Jersey and Pennsylvania. Frank bought large quantities and large varieties of goods direct from the manufacturers and everything was sold for ten cents or less.

Very soon his brother, a cousin and two friends joined him in the venture, but they all ran their stores separately to avoid competing with one another. In 1910 the business was extended to England where goods sold for 3d and 6d (1p and 2½p). In 1912 all these stores, with two owned by the company who backed him originally, were amalgamated to form the F. W. Woolworth company. And the following year, twenty-five years after Frank had set up his counter in his employer's store, with his own money he built the 60-storey Woolworth Building on Broadway, New York City, which at 692ft high was at the time the tallest building in the world.

With his perseverance and self-confidence, Frank Woolworth had added a new dimension to retailing and given the poorer people a chance to choose from a wide variety of goods that they could afford. He was economy conscious himself, almost penny-pinching, and when he died on 8 April 1919 his personal fortune was estimated at 65 million dollars (about 16 million pounds), and his company owned over a thousand stores in the United States and Canada alone.

Eponyms

ANNIE OAKLEY   A complimentary ticket. From Annie Oakley (see p15), markswoman in Buffalo Bill's Wild West Show, who shot holes in playing cards. The holed cards resembled the punched tickets used as complimentaries in the United States of America.

BALACLAVA see CARDIGAN

BANTING   A method of reducing superfluous fat by a protein diet. From William Banting (1797–1878), a London cabinet-maker who recommended it in 1863.

BLOOMERS   Drawers. Originally an outfit of jacket, skirt and peg trousers gathered round the ankles. From Mrs Amelia Bloomer (1818–94), an American Women's Rights campaigner, who introduced the outfit in New York in 1849.

BOBBY or **PEELER**   A policeman. From Sir Robert Peel (1788–1850), British Prime Minister who established London's Metropolitan Police force in 1829 when he was Home Secretary.

BOWDLERIZE   To expurgate. From Thomas Bowdler (1754–1825), a Scottish minister who published an expurgated edition of Shakespeare in 1818 so that he could read it to his family.

BOYCOTT   To protest by ostracism. From Captain Charles Cunningham Boycott, agent for the estates of the Earl of Erne in County Mayo, Ireland, who was so treated by his neighbours in December 1880 when he refused to accept their rent because they had fixed what they would pay themselves.

BRAILLE   A system of raised dots representing letters and figures for use by the blind as a 'reading' aid. From its French inventor, Louis Braille (1809–52).

BROTHER JONATHAN   Someone who knows the answer or can solve a problem. From Jonathan Trumbull, governor of Connecticut during the American War of Independence. George Washington, in need of ammunition, consulted a council of officers. When they could not offer any suggestions, Washington said, 'We must consult brother Jonathan', meaning Trumbull. This he did and Trumbull solved the problem for him.

BROUGHAM   A one-horse closed four-wheel carriage. From Lord Brougham (1778–1868), a British statesman who was often seen riding in one.

BUNSEN   A type of gas burner. From the German chemist, Professor R. W. Bunsen (1811–99), who invented it.

BURKE   To murder by stifling. So (colloquially) to put an end to something quietly. From William Burke (1792–1829) who committed the crime so as sell his victims' bodies for dissection.

CARDIGAN   A knitted jacket first worn by the Earl of Cardigan (1797–1868), who led the famous Charge of the Light Brigade at the Battle of Balaclava, and his men, to protect them from the Russian winter. The **BALACLAVA** helmet originates from the same source.

CHAUVINIST or **CHAUVIN**   An exaggeratedly patriotic person. From Nicolas Chauvin, a French soldier noted for his ardent enthusiasm for Napoleon.

CLERIHEW   A humorous verse, often satirical and biographical, of four uneven rhymed lines. From E. Clerihew Bentley (1875–1956), who originated it in his *Biography for Beginners* (1905).

DERBY   A horse race. From the 12th Earl of Derby (1776–1834) who instituted the Derby Stakes in 1780.

DERRICK   A type of crane for hoisting heavy objects. From a seventeenth century Tyburn hangman named Derrick.

DIESEL   An internal combustion engine. From Rudolf Diesel (1858–1913), the German engineer who invented it.

DOILY A fancy mat used on cake dishes. From a family called Doily or Doyley, haberdashers in the Strand, London, from about 1710 until 1850, who first sold them.

DUNCE From John Duns Scotus, one of the most brilliant of medieval schoolmen. After his death in 1308 his teaching was disparaged by his opponents and anyone who supported his ideas was labelled a Duns or Dunser, meaning a stupid person. The words Dunses or Dunsers eventually became dunces.

GALVANISE To stimulate by electric current. From Luigi Galvani (1737–98), Italian physiologist who discovered the method.

GEORGETTE A fine, semi-transparent crêpe material. From Madame Georgette de la Plante, an early twentieth-century French dressmaker and milliner, who often used such material.

GREENGAGE A type of plum. From Sir William Gage who introduced the fruit into England from France about 1725.

GUILLOTINE Paper-cutting machine. From Dr Joseph Ignace Guillotin (1738–1814), a French physician who proposed the adoption of the decapitation instrument, which was devised by the French surgeon Antoine Louis, in order to prevent unnecessary pain for the victims beheaded during the French Revolution.

GUY An effigy burned on 5 November. An odd-looking fellow. From Guy Fawkes (see p64).

HANSARD The official printed report of the proceedings in Parliament. From Luke Hansard (1752–1828) who first printed it in 1774.

HANSOM A two-wheeled cab. From its inventor, Joseph Aloysius Hansom (1803–82), an architect who designed the Cathedral Church of SS. Mary and Boniface at Plymouth and Birmingham Town Hall.

HEATH ROBINSON An over-ingenious mechanical contraption which is usually too complicated to work. From W. Heath Robinson (1872–1944), an artist who drew such absurdities for the satirical magazine *Punch* and elsewhere.

JOE MILLER A stale joke. From Joe Miller (1684-1738), a popular comedian of that time. In 1739, a John Mottley published a book of old jokes which he unkindly, and without permission, called *Joe Miller's Jest Book*, and the old jokes became known as Joe Millers.

MACADAM A road surface. From John Loudon Macadam (1756-1836), a Scottish surveyor who first introduced it.

MACINTOSH A raincoat made from cloth waterproofed with rubber. From Charles Macintosh (1766-1843), who patented the material in 1823.

MAE WEST Inflatable life-jacket. From the buxom film star, Mae West (1892-1980). So named by British airmen during World War II.

MANSARD A type of roof. From the French architect, François Mansard (1598-1666), who frequently employed it.

MESMERISM A type of hypnotism. From Frederich Anton Mesmer (1734-1815), Austrian physician, who introduced his theory of 'animal magnetism' in Paris in 1778.

MORSE CODE Telegraphic code in which letters are represented by dots and dashes. From its American inventor, Samuel Finley Breese Morse (1791-1872).

PAUL JONES A 'change-partners' dance. From the naval adventurer Paul Jones (1747-92), who frequently left his own ship to seize another, and who was also a fickle lover.

PEELER *See* **BOBBY**

PEEPING TOM Someone who pries on others, especially through windows. From Tom of Coventry, a tailor, who peeped at Lady Godiva (see p84) as she rode naked through the streets in 1040.

PINCHBECK An alloy of copper and zinc resembling gold. So, any cheap or spurious article. From Christopher Pinchbeck (1670-1732), a cheap jewellery and trinket manufacturer in Fleet Street, London.

PLIMSOLL LINE A line marked on a cargo ship indicating the depth to which the ship may be safely loaded in salt water. From Samuel Plimsoll (1824-98), MP for Derby, who campaigned for this in the interest of ships' crews.

PULLMAN   A luxurious railway carriage. From George M. Pullman (1831-97), an American industrialist, who designed it.

QUISLING   A traitor. From Vidkun Quisling (1887-1945), a Norwegian who betrayed his country to the Germans during the German invasion of Norway in 1940, and who was shot as a traitor on 24 October 1945.

RAGLAN   An overcoat without shoulder seams and with sleeves extending to the neck. From Field Marshall Lord Raglan (1788-1855), Commander-in-Chief of the British forces in the Crimean War, who first had this type of coat made from sacks to protect his men against the bitter Russian winter.

SADISM   Cruel perversion. From the Marquis de Sade (1740-1814), French pervert and writer of obscene plays and novels.

SAM BROWNE   A leather belt with a shoulder strap. From its inventor, General Sir Sam Browne, VC (1824-1901), a veteran of the Indian Mutiny.

SANDWICH   From the 4th Earl of Sandwich (1718-92), who would not leave the gambling table to eat and asked the waiter to bring him some ham between two slices of bread which he could eat without stopping play.

SHRAPNEL   A type of shell containing bullets, which scatter by a bursting charge. From General Henry Shrapnel (1761-1842), who invented it during the Peninsular War.

SILHOUETTE   A black-filled shadow-outline. From Etienne de Silhouette (1709-67), French Minister of Finance under Louis XV. His meanness and cheese-paring economies lost him his job and to make a living he made portraits from cheap black paper cut-outs. His idea soon became a craze in Paris and later spread to England.

SPOONERISM   The transposition of initial sounds of words, so making a ludicrous sentence. From Dr William Spooner (see p48).

WATT   A unit of power. From James Watt (1736-1819), Scottish engineer and inventor of the steam engine.

WELLINGTON   Waterproof footwear. From the knee-length riding boots first worn by the Duke of Wellington (see p70) during the Napoleonic Wars.

Index